Women in Chains

Women in Chains

by Wensley Clarkson

BLAKE'S
TRUE
CRIME
LIBRARY

Published by Blake Publishing Ltd,
3 Bramber Court, 2 Bramber Road,
London W14 9PB, England

First published in 2000

ISBN 1 85782 353 2

British Library Cataloguing-in-Publication Data:

A catalogue record for this book is
available from the British Library.

Typeset by t2

Printed in Finland by
WS Bookwell, Juva

1 3 5 7 9 10 8 6 4 2

'I will cut your face. I will kill you and scatter your pieces in the desert if you ever disobey an order. You are my slave. You will do exactly what I say; eat only when I tell you and only what I give you. If you attempt to steal food, you will be starved until I decide you have learned your lesson. You will sleep on the floor outside my bedroom and only for the hours I tell you. You will have no days off and you will not leave this house unaccompanied. Remember, I hold your passport. If the police find you, you will be brought back to me. And if you are, you may be killed. Don't forget — there are plenty more where you came from.'

The threat made to slave Alice Santos, just after she was 'employed' as a domestic in the Middle East in 1992.

Notes of Gratitude

I owe my deepest thanks to all those people who have helped make this book possible. First, to my manager and literary agent Peter Miller, without whom this book would never have happened. His support and guidance have been very much appreciated. His team members Jody, Harrison and Uri also deserve praise. Numerous criminologists, journalists, policemen, social workers, concerned individuals and, most importantly, the families of the subjects themselves provided invaluable assistance — some from as far away as California and Japan.

A special note of thanks to Sergeant Tom Budds of the LA County Sheriff's Department, whose help went beyond the call of duty despite his incredibly heavy workload.

Then there are: John Glatt, Mark Sandelson, Martin Dunn, Nick Ferrari, Tewe Pannier, Simon Kinnersley, Joe Poalella, Sadie Mayne, Rosie Ries, Savage, Charlie Spicer, John Blake, Jon Ryan, Jon Wosnop, Pete Pickton, Viola and Mir.

Also, my eternal thanks to the reference libraries at News International, London and Chief Librarian Fagi at the *Daily News* library in New York, as well as to the *Sunday Times*, *Daily Telegraph*, *Daily Mirror*, the *Sun*, the *News Of The World*, *Daily Star*, *Sunday Mirror* magazine, the *Evening Standard*, the *Mail on Sunday*, the *New Yorker*, the *Los Angeles Times*, *Secret* magazine and the *Leather Journal*.

A special note of thanks to everyone at Kalayaan and Anti-Slavery International for providing details of certain cases as well as their superb booklet entitled *Britain's Secret Slaves*. Also Gordon Thomas's book *Enslaved*, published by Bantam in 1990. And finally, to all other sources of reference material which have proved so inspirational for this book.

The stories of all these women are true. While the words are those of the author, the accounts of these shocking human tragedies come directly from these unfortunate slave girls. In some cases, names have been changed and various events slightly altered to protect the well-being of recognisable individuals. In other instances, these women have been fully identified after speaking out on behalf of the tens of thousands of other slaves throughout today's world.

In telling these true stories, it is not the intention of the author to demean any one group of people: just to reveal a practice that seems a tragic indictment of our so-called civilised society.

Foreword

'In 1833 / The Abolition of Slavery' This is a rhyme that is taught to children across the country, and they have no reason to doubt its accuracy. Or do they?

For this astonishing book, Wensley Clarkson has travelled the world to hunt out stories of women who have been enslaved in the cruellest ways possible. Some of the instances he has found are from the furthest-flung backwaters; alarmingly, he has found plenty of instances on our very doorstep. Even in the so-called civilised countries of the world — England, America, Japan — he has found terrible examples of this vicious trade.

Some of the women you will read about in this book have led lives of sexual slavery; for others it has been domestic. What all the stories have in common, however, is that they are perfectly, shockingly true ...

Adam Parfitt
Editor
Blake's True Crime Library

Contents

Preface

Workers have been transferred in large numbers and over long distances since the end of the fifteenth century, from the enslavement of indigenous peoples, through African slavery, following the conquest of the Americas, right up to the present day.

However, today, in 1996, although the world officially condemns slavery, laws in many countries still consider domestic staff to be household members and this non-recognition renders them liable to abuse. It legitimises slavery.

The conclusion of the Gulf War did not bring any improvement to the lot of domestic servants in that region. In 1994, there were estimated to be thousands of women slaves hiding in foreign embassies in Kuwait City following outrageous violence against them. Most cannot leave the country because their passports were 'confiscated' by their employers.

The status of women in certain Gulf States is thought to be a crucial factor in the treatment of slave girls. They have no right to vote and are still expected to be docile and subservient to their husbands. As the cases highlighted in this book will illustrate, it is all too often women who are the most brutal employers when it comes to the abuse of female servants. Many experts believe that this is because they are 'passing on' elements of their own brutal treatment at the hands of husbands and reclaiming an element of power which is denied to them in all other areas of their life.

Sexual and physical abuse is meted out by many

nationalities: American, British, Indian, German, Nigerian, Spanish and South African, to name but a few. And it frequently takes place in the rich neighbourhoods of some of the most sophisticated cities in the world.

There have been numerous cases of the slavery and imprisonment of women so that they can be used as sexual toys, often with tragic results. These women are beaten, starved and face non-stop physical and sexual abuse. At night, many are chained to their beds to prevent escape.

One of the biggest problems is in London, where the wealthy in areas like Hampstead, Mayfair, Knightsbridge, Chelsea and Kensington employ an estimated FIVE THOUSAND female domestic slaves. The women themselves come from all over the developing world, including Sri Lanka, India, Nigeria, Sierra Leone, North Africa, and some poorer European nations.

However, the largest recorded number come from the Philippines, via the Gulf States.

Employers have a special dispensation to bring these domestic servants into the United States, Britain and other countries under one of two categories: as 'visitors' or as 'persons named to work with a specified employer'. Immigration officials in Britain — where the slavery problem has reached epidemic proportions — have even been issued with highly confidential guidelines which allow any domestic who has been employed for at least twelve months to continue her employment in the United Kingdom. The guidelines clearly state that if a domestic leaves her original employer before twelve months have passed, she is deemed an illegal immigrant in the eyes of the law.

In the United States, immigration rules which permit employers to bring domestic servants into the country providing they continue working for them, have also opened the floodgates to abuse and slavery. Many of these women are abused behind the closed doors of so-called 'respectable' homes.

Domestic servants arriving from the Third World or countries with brutal regimes into countries like Britain and the United States naturally expect freedom at last to prevail. They presume they will be able to choose whatever job they want and walk away from the horrors inflicted on them by brutal employers. But none of them realise that a slave who has run away from an employer has no legal rights.

For the cruel truth about life as a domestic servant in many countries is that as soon as the work visa with their current employer expires, they automatically become illegal immigrants in the eyes of the law. In other words, if they run away from cruel employers they are automatically thrown out of the country. It is an archaic situation that encourages the continuing abuse of domestics.

Employers of slave girls recognise this, and frequently threaten their workers with dire consequences if they dare to escape.

In any case, fleeing is not easy. There are practical difficulties: doors are kept bolted, windows locked and barred and there may even be security guards or dogs patrolling the premises. Many women are simply not allowed out of the house, so they have no idea where they are, where to go, or how to get there. They have no money, no papers, no friends, no belongings. It is a leap into the unknown, and always there is the fear that their employers will discover what they are planning.

Recent moves by various governments to make employers set out in writing the main terms and conditions of employment before allowing them to bring an employee into a country have done little to stem the influx of slave girls. What most employers promise in writing bears little resemblance to the way they intend to treat their servants.

Great Britain, the United States and the Gulf States, among others, all claim they are making further moves to alleviate the plight of the slave girls. Officials insist they are planning changes to the work permit rules that have been open to abuse by the rich who are able to employ servants as slaves.

But these governments all say they can do little to prevent the abuse and humiliation of slave girls because most of the girls are terrified that if they report their employers they will themselves be deported.

Slave girls remain hidden from the outside world in tiny cupboards or bedrooms, sometimes even bare floors on isolated hallways. They are treated like dirt and regularly abused by their 'respectable' masters and mistresses.

This book is a testimony to the indomitable spirit and great courage of these women, many of whom have spoken out for the first time, risking the full wrath of the people they have served in fear.

Hearts live by being wounded.
Oscar Wilde

Suffering is permanent, obscure and dark
And shares the nature of infinity.
William Wordsworth, 1795

Slave n.

1.   A person legally owned by another and having no freedom of action or right to property.
2.   A person who is forced to work for another against his will.
3.   A person under the domination of another person or some habit or influence.
4.   A person who works in harsh conditions for low pay.

Dictionary definition

1

Sisters of Terror

*'Freedom is indivisible, and when one man is enslaved,
all are not free.'*

John F Kennedy 1963

Mayfair, Central London, early 1980s.

Princesses Simiya and Faria al-Sabah — half-sisters
of the Emir of Kuwait — were considered strangely
exotic creatures on London's West End nightclub
circuit.

They were ostentatiously wealthy — designer
dresses, expensive hairstyling and manicure sessions, and
an abundance of gold necklaces, bracelets and rings.

But beneath the glitter and glamour lay the minds
of two sadists who spent part of every day for four years
severely punishing their personal slave girl.

Laxmi Peria Swami still does not know her own age, and her careworn face and the black circles under her eyes make it difficult to guess, but she is probably in her fifties now. The two princesses refused to tell her how old she was. They preferred to taunt and punish her. They loved to make her feel as if she had no right to any life outside the four walls of their luxurious London home.

This particular day had started just like any other for Laxmi during her employment in that appalling household. The two princesses had stayed in bed until around midday after yet another night on the town, something they would never have dared to do back in their native Kuwait. Simiya and Faria had hardly had time to adjust their eyes to the midday sun when they decided it was time for Laxmi to earn her keep.

They did not take into consideration the fact that Laxmi had been standing and waiting for them while they were out nightclubbing the previous evening. She had to do that every time her mistresses went out.

'Stand on this spot and do not move until we return,' Faria told her slave girl when they first began going out until the early hours after arriving in London from Kuwait.

By the time Laxmi got to her tiny cubby-hole by the kitchen, it would be fair to say that she was probably even more exhausted than the two spoilt Arab princesses. Her 'home' was a strip of cold wooden floor in a passageway by the kitchen, with a two-inch-thick mattress and little else in the way of comfort.

'I need a massage,' hissed Simiya at Laxmi as she stretched her arms in the sunlight which was peeping through a slight gap in the silky curtains of her interior-designed bedroom. Her sister turned over and slipped back into a light slumber on the bed next to her.

Laxmi took a deep breath and pulled up the sleeves of her cheap cotton smock.

'Wash your hands first. I don't know where they've been.'

Laxmi did not reply but walked towards the en suite bathroom. She had long since learned that she should never respond to the sisters unless they asked her a specific question.

'Not in there, you idiot. In the kitchen,' muttered Simiya contemptuously.

By the time Laxmi returned a few minutes later, Simiya was lying on the soft mattress gossiping to a girlfriend on the phone. She did not even look up when Laxmi appeared by her side.

Instead, Simiya rolled over on to her stomach, spread her legs slightly and just lay there in her pink satin nightgown waiting to be pampered.

'Oh, this guy was so beautiful. I could have eaten him on the spot,' she giggled to her friend on the phone. 'His eyes were so blue ... COME ON!'

Laxmi rolled up the long satin nightdress so that it exposed the cellulite-ridden thighs of her mistress. A slightly unpleasant aroma wafted through the air, but it was nothing compared with what she had experienced since arriving in London with the princesses.

'So,' Simiya continued to her girlfriend, 'I played it really cool with him, you know. Hold on a minute.'

Simiya turned and looked up at Laxmi. 'Harder. Do it harder!'

Laxmi did as her mistress commanded.

'Not that fucking hard.'

Laxmi eased off, aware that she had momentarily allowed herself to betray her inner feelings.

Outside the house — on the busy, civilised streets of Mayfair — the rich and beautiful were shopping in the exclusive stores of Piccadilly, unaware that a poor, innocent, illiterate slave girl was being bullied and tormented in a life that could have come straight out of a novel by Dickens.

As Simiya continued babbling on the phone like some adolescent schoolgirl, Laxmi allowed her mind to drift back to the days when she was a poverty-stricken, but happy, young woman with her four young children on the streets of Dehli.

Here she was, trapped in a palace of misery thousands of miles from her offspring, whom she had been prevented from contacting for the best part of four years. Laxmi did not even know her children's location. Occasionally, one of the older ones would write to her and, if she was lucky, the princesses would read the letters to her. But she had no actual address for them.

Suddenly, the slave girl was snapped out of her daydream by the crunching pain of a stiletto heel smashing into her shin. It was Faria.

'Put more effort into it,' she spat at Laxmi.

On the bed, Simiya was still talking to her girlfriend on the phone, but a sneer came to her lips when she saw her sister kicking their slave girl.

Laxmi tried her hardest to respond to her orders, but she was clearly exhausted. Unfortunately, her weary expression simply fuelled the two sisters' rage.

'I said, do it harder,' yelled Faria at their servant.

As Laxmi increased the pressure, her hands sinking into the folds of the flesh at the back of her mistresses' thighs, Simiya sighed. It could have been a sign of pleasure or perhaps just the pure satisfaction of knowing that she was in complete and utter control of another human being. Whatever the cause, those two sisters were on the ultimate power trip. They owned every inch of Laxmi and they would never let her forget it.

Laxmi tried not to think about the possible sexual implications of many of her duties for the princesses. She did not question many of their requests for the sort of massages that seemed to have little to do with aching bones and more to do with sexual pleasure.

Just then, Simiya turned over on to her back and instructed Laxmi to pull up her nightgown entirely. Neither of the sisters had any inhibitions about their bodies in front of their slave girl. They considered Laxmi to be subhuman so her emotions and feelings never once came into the equation. She was expected to wash and massage every inch of their bodies.

Faria sat down on the plush bedroom armchair and examined her perfectly manicured pink fingernails as Laxmi continued to massage her sister's body.

'Hurry up, we need to be at that restaurant opposite Harrods by one,' she commented matter-of-factly.

Laxmi wondered to herself why on earth Faria had kicked her as she massaged her sister. She thought perhaps it was a show of strength on the part of the older sister. Faria did it to her virtually every time she was attending to Simiya. She also noticed that Faria was nearly always fully dressed when she lashed out. Those black patent stilettos, or similar shoes would always be the first instruments of pain. Laxmi had never dared asked her why she was being beaten. It had just become a habit.

'She's so pathetic. Look at her.' Faria did not even bother looking up from her nails as she started to castigate her slave girl.

Just then, she eased up her pencil skirt, exposing three inches of thigh, pulled her leg back and aimed her spiky heel directly at Laxmi's backside.

Faria laughed, 'There's certainly not much to sink my foot into.'

Twenty minutes later, Faria and Simiya were just about to depart when they decided to give some last minute orders to their slave girl.

'You won't have time for lunch,' Faria said, coldly. Then Simiya chipped in, 'Make sure you throw away all the remains from dinner last night.'

As an afterthought, she added, 'Pour some drink over them and then put them in the dustbins outside.'

That was the cruellest order of all. It was even worse than the sadistic beatings as far as Laxmi was concerned, for it meant that she could not eat any of the remains of the Harrods-catered cuisine that had been half wasted by the eight guests who had been round at the house for lunch the previous day.

Sometimes, Laxmi would be so starving that she would stretch through the kitchen window to grab something from the dustbins to satisfy her craving for some real food.

The only liquid Laxmi was ever allowed was water

from the tap in the tiny maid's bathroom next to that cold passageway by the kitchen. Most nights, Laxmi would curl up on a paper-thin mattress hours after the princesses had gone to bed, having ensured that the entire house was spotlessly clean so that they would not attack her the moment they woke the next morning.

Laxmi could not remember a night when she had not cried herself to sleep since arriving in London. Her dreams were the only escape from the pain and anguish of reality. She would find herself back in India with the children in the middle of the countryside, smiling faces, happy, contented. But then something would happen and those dreams would turn into horrific nightmares that usually woke Laxmi with a terrible start and snapped her cruelly back to reality.

A few hours later, Laxmi would find herself standing in front of those two evil mistresses, awaiting her first punishment of the day. This usually consisted of a punch in the stomach or a kick to the kidneys if she was even a few seconds late in waking them up.

Although Laxmi was never actually shackled, she felt an enormous psychological pressure not even to contemplate leaving the princesses. They would frequently warn her that if she ever ran away, the Kuwaiti secret police would track her down and kill her. Laxmi had no reason to doubt them and it terrified her. She convinced herself that it was her fate to stay trapped in that house of horrors for the rest of her life.

At least when the princesses read her children's letters to her, they seemed to be showing some compassion. But Laxmi did not realise that those letters simply represented another piece of their twisted, sadistic behaviour.

Both of them had taken to making up entire sections of the letters just to tease and taunt their slave girl — and to ensure that she would never leave their employment.

Once, they told her that her beloved son had been killed in a motorbike accident. It was a cruel hoax on the part of the sisters, but Laxmi was not to know that. She burst into tears as soon as they started telling her about the 'tragedy'.

The sisters' response was predictably brutal. 'Shut up!' they snarled.

But, for once, Laxmi could not obey their command. She was so distraught by the news that she became even more hysterical.

Faria walked towards her. Perhaps she was going to break the habit of a lifetime and show some compassion? The rings on her fingers made the first backhanded slap particularly painful for Laxmi. The three or four hits that followed were dulled by the slave girl's deeply emotional state.

When she had finished, Faria turned to Simiya.

'It's your turn.'

Simiya giggled childishly and stood up. She must have just caught the look of fear in Laxmi's eyes as she clenched her fist for the first punch.

Eventually, Laxmi stopped crying, but the tears inside her would never dry up. She suffered the beating in just the same way she had suffered everything over the previous four years — with complete numbness. She had become so used to being abused that she had stopped wondering why it was happening. She did not notice the smiles of satisfaction on the faces of her two mistresses as they tried to beat the spirit out of their slave girl for ever.

Many years later, Laxmi discovered that her son had not died in that 'crash'.

Laxmi was not the only slave girl working for the brutal princesses. The other servant in the household, a Sri Lankan called Shamsu, was badly burned when she was forced to place her hand directly on to an electric ring on the cooker.

The princesses were about to make Laxmi do the same, but one of them pointed out, 'If we do that, we won't have anyone left to do the housework.'

Laxmi was particularly haunted by one awful incident that had occurred when she first started working for the princesses in Kuwait, before they began the regular trips to their luxurious home in London.

She was taken to see three men who were being publicly hanged and both the princesses told her, 'If you do anything wrong, this is what will happen to you.'

Laxmi never doubted their word.

In fact, throughout her employment with the princesses, her tiny wages had been withheld, even though they were supposed to send them on to her family in India.

The princesses treated Laxmi and Shamsu like luggage as they accompanied the royal party to and from London, where the two mistresses were free from the strict religious restrictions imposed on them in Kuwait. After one particularly brutal incident during which both of the princesses turned on Laxmi and tried to strangle her with wire flex, Laxmi managed to escape from the house when the front door — which was usually permanently locked — was accidentally left open. She ran into the street, crying and bleeding, and a passing taxi took her to the Indian High Commission, which then sent her back to the princesses because she did not have any money to pay for her airfare back to India.

After that abortive escape attempt, the princesses began punishing Laxmi even more regularly. They also denied her all freedom of movement — doors and windows to the house were barred from the outside — and the princesses established complete dominance over Laxmi, ensuring her absolute obedience.

Laxmi continued to sleep in the passageway outside the kitchen, but now it was always locked. She was not allowed any clothes of her own and she was given nothing other than the occasional scrap of bread. Whenever she was caught taking food from the dustbin, she would be beaten by either or both of the princesses. Initially they used a broomstick, but then one day Faria appeared in the kitchen brandishing a horsewhip and started lashing out at Laxmi's bottom.

'You will only eat when we tell you. Do you understand?'

Laxmi nodded weakly.

'Now bend over.'

Sometimes the princesses would come back from riding in Hyde Park and find some excuse or other to punish Laxmi, although it seemed more likely that they were getting some sort of thrill out of whipping their slave girl while dressed in jodhpurs and black leather boots.

Occasionally, the princesses would use knotted electric flex just to vary the form of punishments they meted out. By this time, slave girls Laxmi and Shamsu was banned from talking to each other and if they were ever spotted in conversation they could take it for granted that a severe beating would follow.

But probably the worst incident of all occurred when the princesses accused Laxmi of not cleaning the house properly

'You're filthy. You stink. You're pathetic,' they started taunting their slave girl.

Then one of the princesses started squinting at Laxmi.

'I want that gold in your mouth.'

Laxmi did not reply. She feared she knew what was coming next.

The princesses then produced a huge pair of pliers. One of them held her down and the other started some dental removal work. Somehow, the screams that filled the house that evening escaped the attention of any of the princesses' neighbours.

Eventually, the other servant, Shamsu, escaped from the house with the help of a local Indian from whom she had begged scraps of food when she was starving. He felt sorry for her and told her to go to the Sri Lankan High Commission. There, for the first time, the full story of the horrific regime under the two princesses was revealed.

Sri Lankan officials alerted the police to the plight of Laxmi, who was still living in the house.

When a group of policemen from Paddington Green station, led by Detective Sergeant Steve Gaskin, entered the princesses' house with a search warrant to rescue her, Laxmi was terrified and at first refused to go with them. She thought they had come on the princesses' orders to hang her.

The police eventually persuaded her to leave with them and they took her to a refuge in Brent, north-west London, where she began to receive counselling for the horrendous years she had spent in captivity.

One of the first things the police did was ask a doctor to examine Laxmi. He found ninety-seven scars on her body, some of which, he said, would never heal. Her eyes had also been damaged when one of the princesses had thrown a set of keys at her face.

Laxmi was seen by an ophthalmologist, a dentist — who found clear evidence of the removal of those two gold teeth — and a psychiatrist. The evidence of all these experts was to prove crucial in the years ahead. Their findings substantiated Laxmi's claims when the case finally reached the civil courts five years later.

Long before that, criminal proceedings were initiated, but the two princesses denied the main charges of grievous bodily harm, actual bodily harm and conspiracy to cause bodily harm. By the time the case came to Knightsbridge Crown Court in 1985, many of these charges had been dropped. Some suspected that this was a direct attempt to placate the Kuwaiti Government. The princesses were eventually given six-month suspended sentences and Laxmi was awarded compensation: £260 on one count and £1,500 for another — sums which, to princesses from one of the richest families in the world, were small change.

Laxmi was livid that they had got off with such light punishment and sought fresh legal advice to start civil proceedings against her former mistresses. There then followed six years of hard slog, many setbacks, and a case of astonishing complexity

Laxmi's lawyer, Rohit Sanghvi, began work on her case by looking back through more than a century of cases, searching for precedents. There were none. No servant in Britain had ever brought a successful action against an employer for unlawful imprisonment and grievous bodily harm.

In the case of the Kuwaiti princesses, there was another problem — finding them. Laxmi could not supply an address in Kuwait and they also owned homes elsewhere. The police needed their home address in the Middle East in order to serve the arrest warrant because they were away for such long periods.

There were problems for Laxmi, too. Her allegations had to be substantiated. She had undergone a series of physical examinations for medical reports, not only by experts from her own side, but experts for her employers, too, seeking to undermine her claims. For a deeply modest, nervous woman these examinations were an ordeal.

The tactics of the princesses and their lawyers were simply to try to wear Laxmi down; to destroy her ability to go through with the case. They were obstructive at every stage of the legal proceedings. Until just before the civil case was due to be heard, they denied all charges — even those to which they had already pleaded guilty in the criminal court — and even claimed that the two servants had beaten each other.

Finally, the princesses realised that even they — members of one of the richest and most powerful dynasties in the Middle East — were not immune to the persistence of a dedicated lawyer and an unshakable witness whose body will bear the evidence of their cruelty for the rest of her life.

For her pain and suffering at the time, and for her continued suffering afterwards, for her nightmares, terror, trauma and unlawful imprisonment, Laxmi was awarded £300,000 by a High Court jury on 8 December, 1989. To this was added a further £19,200 in interest to cover the delays. Legal aid costs of about £100,000 were awarded against the princesses, whose own legal bill amounted to at least three times as much.

It will come as no surprise to learn that it took a further year to get the money from the princesses. Ironically, if it had not been for Iraq's invasion of Kuwait, and the country's need for Western support, it might never have been paid.

As for Laxmi, she does not doubt that it was all worthwhile.

'After the long struggle, I feel I was entitled to what I got as recompense for all my pain.'

She then looked into the distance, unsmiling.

'To them, the money is nothing, it's like air; but it's my body they abused and every scar on my body reminds me of what I went through. No amount of money was worth that.

'What matters to me is that the truth of my story has been recognised; that I was believed by the judge and jury — that was what mattered. It was a vindication

— I was believed, and not the princesses. I could have just died in this country, and nobody would have known or cared and for all we know, many others do die.'

2

Flower from the Heavens

'No one shall be held in slavery or servitude; slavery and the slave trade shall be prohibited in all their forms.'

Article 4 Of The Universal Declaration Of Human Rights, 1948

Rongmung Road, Bangkok, Thailand, Summer, 1989. Frightened faces peer from sordid shop-fronts that have become prisons for hundreds of young girls waiting to be sold into a life of drudgery and degradation. This district is probably the most notorious centre for slavery in the world.

The street has an atmosphere of dread and danger. The innocent faces wait to be sold like items in a market. They will be raped and abused and will most probably die before they are 30.

Beady-eyed western men prowl the street

inspecting the available 'goods'. Many of them will buy a child to satisfy their lust and perverted desires. Two weeks later, the same battered and bewildered girls will be dumped back on Rongmung Road where they will once again be forced to try and catch the attention of yet another master.

A cycle of poverty and desperation is mainly responsible for this appalling scenario. The child often becomes too expensive for her parents to maintain so she is passed on to a brothel or sweatshop where she can earn her keep.

Many of the girls are as young as twelve years old. Their impoverished parents sell them on to shady figures like sadistic Madam Paan Unkham. They receive no money from the brothel-keeper, just a promise that their daughters will eventually be sold on to a westerner who will give them the sort of life they could never enjoy on the backstreets of Bangkok.

The going price for a little girl is $200 (£130), but the number of pretty young, female sex slaves available on Rongmung Road means that it could be many months before they are bought. Many will end up chained and abused by heartless sex fiends intent on finding 'fresh meat'.

Many of the slave girls are put to work in the brothels that service the hundreds of thousands of western visitors to the city's red-light district, a place where intercourse with children as young as eight is openly available.

The so-called lucky ones are put to work in sweatshops where they receive virtually no wages except for a roof over their heads and a few scraps of food each day. Often, their parents get a small cash payment each month, but this is minimal.

One such available slave girl was twelve-year-old Tatip Chauthon. Her beaming, innocent face soon attracted attention on the seedy Rongmung strip. She watched in horror as some of her friends were sold either to sexually depraved men or on to the so-called 'baby brothels' that are dotted all over Bangkok.

Tatip emerged from the shadows into the burning heat of the midday sun ... a little girl lost, lonely and frightened. She was on sale to the highest bidder — as a personal slave to a sweatshop owner, if she was lucky, or to a sex pervert if she was not.

By the end of the 1980s, it was estimated that a staggering 800,000 girls under the age of fifteen had been coerced into working as child prostitutes in Bangkok.

Hundreds of the girls fall into the hands of pimps even before they reach the age of puberty, and one child welfare spokesman in Bangkok claimed, 'I don't think Thailand has any virgins left over the age of thirteen.'

Not surprisingly, doctors believe the country's current AIDS epidemic has been mainly caused by the depraved behaviour of callous men towards these innocent children.

Tatip had been sold by her parents and stood, waiting, in one of the shops on a grubby sidestreet just off the main drag. But no one made an offer to buy her, even though the slave dealers — who call themselves 'labour agents' — confidently predicted that they would sell her 'very quickly' and pass on a commission to her family.

As the days turned into weeks and no offers were forthcoming, Tatip was allowed to take a position further back in the shop, thus avoiding many of the potential buyers.

The irony of the situation was that her family would probably not receive any more than a mere pittance from the dealers — and the children themselves often worked for nothing after being told that their wages had been paid directly to their parents.

The open abuse of the system is clear to everyone, but little or nothing is ever done by the Thai authorities. Tatip's 'owner' was a woman called Kitiya. She did not care to whom she sold the young girl as long as they paid the going rate of $200. 'You can do what you like with her. She's a good girl. She will obey your commands,' Kitiya told one prospective buyer.

But Tatip was one of the lucky ones. She was bought by a British journalist, Peter Bond, who was writing an article on slavery for his London newspaper, the *Daily Star*.

The *Star* helped to expose the evil trade in girl slaves, but sadly their efforts have done little to reduce the alarming number of children still on sale along the Rongmung Road.

The newspaper also exposed the primitive jungle trail that was used to transport children across the Mekong River to Thailand.

Peter Bond was appalled when little Tatip was offered for $200. 'She's twelve years old and her name means "Flower from the Heavens". She is yours,' said slave trader Madam Unkham during the sales pitch of Tatip to reporter Peter Bond on behalf of the dealer,

Kitiya. She claimed that the 5,500 baht ($200) included Tatip's first year's wages, and that there was no need to pay her another penny for the following twelve months. Bond was given a bogus receipt for Tatip. It claimed she was Thai while, in fact, she had been illegally smuggled over the border from Laos. Kitiya had declared a false address for the little girl and claimed she was fourteen. But then no one ever checked the details. Tatip was just another slave girl — nobody would care.

Tatip's life would undoubtedly have been ruined if she had not escaped the clutches of Kitiya and Madam Unkham.

Tatip was eventually sold to Bond with nothing more than the shabby clothes she wore and a polythene bag containing a spare, cheap cotton skirt.

She was tired, hungry and filthy after her gruelling three-day journey from her home deep in the Laos jungle.

When Bond took her out for a meal later, she admitted she had never seen such food, but could hardly eat anything. It then emerged that all she had ever eaten in her village were snakes, frogs, beetles, fish and fried rice. She then explained why her parents had sold her. 'They have no money and with no rain it's difficult for them to find something to eat.'

Tatip told Bond that she had heard strange rumours about other children in neighbouring villages who had disappeared. But she could not believe that her parents had actually sold her.

'I don't want to see them again after what they have done to me,' she explained.

After being brought to the banks of the Mekong

with six other girls, Tatip and her friends were handed over to the evil Madam Unkham, who took charge of the terrified children in order to sell them on the streets of Bangkok.

But before setting out on that journey, Unkham drummed into them what to say if questioned by a policeman or prospective buyer. They had to swear that they came from a Thai village called Navang, where Unkham actually lived.

'None of us knew what was going to happen here, except that we were being sold,' explained Tatip.

Tragically, this is an all too common occurrence in rural Thailand and Laos, where children are sold by their parents to pay debts when a crop fails or their rent increases. Yet it is strictly against Thai law for children or adults to be brought into the country and sold for work. Tatip had lived such an isolated life until her trip to Thailand that she had absolutely no knowledge of the outside world. She had never heard of Europe or America, TV, pop music or electricity. She had seen a few cars, but had never ridden in one. At twelve years old, the youngster had never had an ice-cream or a single toy to play with.

Occasionally, she had seen aeroplanes, but never thought anything of them. She said, 'They were just things in the air. They didn't mean anything and they didn't harm us.'

Tatip had only had two years of formal education — most of the time, she helped her father in the paddy fields near her home. He made less than $5 (£3) a month.

The little slave girl's home was a wooden house

built on stilts. 'We all lived and slept in one big room. I was happy there. But then my mother told me I would have to go away and work. She said she would get money for me. She told me I would have to work very hard for the man who took me to Bangkok.'

Children like Tatip, trapped in Thailand's thousands of brothels and sweatshops, often persevere under appalling conditions because they are frightened of letting their families down. They are also afraid that any money already paid out for them will have to be returned if they flee from a ruthless employer.

Tatip is now living with the family of child welfare expert Kamron Gunatilaka until her future is decided. Mr Gunatilaka said, 'She will remain in our care and only go back to her family when she is old enough to make that decision for herself. No pressure will be put on her.' Officially, Tatip was classed as an illegal immigrant — but she avoided deportation since she told officials that she did not want to go home.

Tatip has been taught to read and write, and has had little trouble learning as she is fairly intelligent. 'Hopefully, she can learn a trade and find her way in the world,' added Mr Gunatilaka.

Postscript: Many other disturbing slave girl cases have emerged in Thailand in recent years.

Recently, more than twenty girls were rescued from a Bangkok sweatshop where they worked in strict silence from 6am to midnight, and were beaten mercilessly if they broke the rules.

In one backstreet, girls making mosquito nets were slashed across the head with heavy scissors for any minor infringement. Other young girls are known to have been burned, whipped, starved, chained up, raped and kept in cupboards for days on end.

In most sweatshops, young girls are forced to eat, sleep and work in the same stuffy, overcrowded room. Toiling for between sixteen to eighteen hours a day, seven days a week, is normal practice. And any slave girl who dares to spend more than three minutes in a stench-ridden toilet can expect a thorough beating.

Many of the sweatshops have barred windows and doors to prevent escape. Crooked policemen profit by accepting bribes and turning a blind eye.

For the desperate youngsters, suicide is often the only way out. As child welfare campaigner Kamron Gunatilaka explained, 'Until there is concentrated and positive action, I'm afraid that more and more children will be sold into this terrible slavery.'

In 1990, Thailand's Government backed new moves to clamp down on child slave racketeers — even so, the legal age for child workers was only raised to thirteen.

3

Cellar of Horror

*'Slavery they can have anywhere. It is a weed that
grows in every soil.'*

Edmund Burke, 1775

3520, North Marshall Street, Philadelphia, 26
November, 1986.

The house was nondescript. For blocks around, in
all directions, there was nothing but rows of houses in
street after street of grim, delapidated dwellings lying on
their bellies with their chins in the street. But Gary
Heidnik's house was different. It was not only set back a
dozen yards from the sidewalk, but it was also detached
on one side, leaving enough space for a small yard and a
driveway up to that rarest of structures in this
neighbourhood — a garage.

It was a ramshackle building made of badly weathered board topped with a row of barbed wire to keep trespassers from climbing over from the alley.

Heidnik had even lined the inside of the creaky doors with metal after a group of neighbourhood punks had fired several shots at the building the previous summer. One of the bullets had damaged Heidnik's Cadillac and that had upset him very much because he was particularly proud of his cars. He kept a 1971 Rolls Royce, which he had bought for $17,000 (£11,000) the previous year.

Inside the house, 43-year-old Gary Heidnik had just brought prostitute Josefina Rivera back for sex — or so she thought. After ten minutes of inactivity in bed together, Heidnik started choking the girl until she almost passed out.

Then he handcuffed her hands behind her back and marched her down to the basement of the house where he forced her down into a cold, damp, dimly-lit room that smelled of mildew and dust. The chill air reminded Rivera that she was wearing nothing but a shirt at the time.

Heidnik then manoeuvered her towards a lumpy, bare mattress which was pushed into one corner of the room. He picked up a small cardboard box and extracted from it a metal rod that had been bent in the middle to form a skinny 'U'. Looking closely, Rivera saw that each end of the rod was threaded. Actually, the device was a commercially made product called a muffler clamp.

Heidnik ran one end of the clamp through a heavy chain, which he pulled from another box, and then forced the clamp over Rivera's ankle. A small metal bar fitted between the two prongs to seal off the open end of the 'U'. He dug in the box again and came up with two nuts, which he screwed into the threads after first moistening them with super glue. From out of nowhere, it seemed, he pulled a hair dryer and aimed that at the glue to make it dry faster. Then he repeated the procedure with a second clamp.

While Rivera lay there frozen with shock, Heidnik flipped the loose end of the chain over a five-inch-thick pipe that came out of the ceiling and ran across the room into the opposite wall.

Standing back to survey his handiwork, Heidnik nodded with satisfaction. 'Sit down,' he told her pointing at the mattress.

When she did, he stretched out beside her, put his head in her naked lap and went to sleep ...

Josefina Rivera woke the following morning to find herself still shackled and naked from the waist down, and very cold. The floor and walls of the basement were bare concrete.

She refused Heidnik's offer of an egg sandwich and orange juice for breakfast in case he had poisoned it.

Then Heidnik began digging a hole in an exposed section of the floor. Rivera feared that it would become her grave, but he had other ideas. Heidnik told the girl that he felt it was time he had a wife and family.

'I want to capture ten women, keep them here and make them all pregnant. Then, when they have babies, I want to raise those children here, too. We'll be one big, happy family.'

Rivera shivered. He did not have to tell her that

she was Number One. Shortly afterwards, he unzipped his trousers and ordered her to take his penis in her mouth. After a few minutes, he forced her to have sex. Her enslavement had begun.

Later that day, Rivera tried to escape but was hauled back into the hole in the ground of the basement which Heidnik had dug earlier. He dragged a piece of plywood over the hole and balanced several bags of dirt on it so that she could not move it. Rivera was bent double so that her chin was on her chest.

Heidnik returned a few minutes later with a radio which he tuned into a heavy-rock station. He left and did not return for twenty-seven hours. Rivera knew precisely how long it was because the station's deejays were fanatical about announcing the time.

Not long afterwards, another girl called Sandra Lindsay was captured by Heidnik and shackled in the dingy cellar beside Rivera.

Since the only article of clothing they were allowed to wear was a thin shirt, the two girls often huddled together for warmth and pleaded for blankets and more clothing. Even worse than the cold was the lack of contact with the outside world, the constant sexual desires of their captor and the ever-present threat of beatings if they disobeyed his orders. Heidnik even tacked soundproofing material to the ceiling of the basement to muffle the noise they made during these regular beatings.

He occasionally served them oatmeal for breakfast. But usually it was Pop-tarts, crackers and white bread. Dinner was rice and shrivelled hot dogs. Sometimes he gave them fried chicken as a treat.

On the sexual front, it became clear that Heidnik's primary aim was to get them pregnant and each day he would demand sex from both of them.

Soon after their imprisonment, Heidnik screwed a large eye-hook into a ceiling beam about seven feet off the floor. If one of them misbehaved, he would put a handcuff on one wrist and slip the other handcuff through the eye-hook. The woman being punished would have to stand for hours on end, with one arm above her head, unable to lie down, sit, or even shift position.

Shortly after this, a girl called Lisa Thomas was captured by Heidnik and taken down to the cellar to join the other two women. Then came Deborah Johnson Dudley.

As the number of inmates grew, a pecking order developed. Rivera — the most streetwise of the group — was learning how to manipulate the manipulator. As time went on, she was punished less frequently than the others and gradually won Heidnik's trust.

One of Heidnik's favourite tactics was to pick one of the group to be in charge when he left them alone, a sort of officer-of-the-day approach. Later, he would come back and ask this supervisor who had misbehaved so that he could dole out punishiment. Discipline usually involved being whacked with the shovel handle, but it also included a restricted diet, time in the 'hole' or being handcuffed to the eye-hook. If the one in charge claimed no one had misbehaved, Heidnik punished her.

Frequently he made them beat each other, and if the woman administering the punishment was not doing it vigorously enough, he would reverse the roles. Or he would take over himself.

Heidnik's sexual appetite showed no sign of declining. It was a rare day when he did not force at least one of the women to have sex with him. Sometimes he would go from one to the other, like a bee pollinating a plant, until he finally climaxed or grew tired. Later, he even forced the women to have sex with each other.

Hygiene was minimal. Heidnik had installed an Elsam for the women to use and he gave them tampons. But in the early days he refused to let them bathe. They had to clean themselves with disposable baby wipes. One day Thomas accidently pulled two of the towels out of the container, sending Heidnik into a rage. Accusing her of wasting property, he laid into her with a shovel handle.

Later on he relented and every day would take one of his prisoners upstairs to wash. They always carried their chains with them, even into the bathtub. After they had soaked for a few minutes, Heidnik would push them on to the bed and have sex with them.

Although the cleanliness situation improved a little, the food situation deteriorated.

One day Heidnik was feeding his two dogs — a huge part-Labrador called Bear and a scruffy collie mutt named Flaky — when he had an idea: the next time one of the women needed to be punished, he grabbed a can of chicken-flavoured dog food and ordered them all to eat.

They balked. 'Eat or take a beating,' he commanded. They ate it. From then on, dog food became a regular part of their diet. Later on it would acquire an even grislier aspect.

By late January, 1987, a fifth girl had been captured by Heidnik and shackled in the cellar alongside his other women. Jacquelyn Askins, a petite, soft-spoken eighteen-year-old, had such small ankles that he had to use a pair of handcuffs on her legs.

Soon after this Sandra Lindsay died after being hung for too long from the eye-hook by handcuffs. Her death presented a major problem for Heidnik. It not only set back his plan to collect a group of human baby machines, but it also meant that he had to figure out what to do with her body. If he put it somewhere and it was found, she could be identified. And if she was identified, she could be traced to him. Now and then, he heard that her sister and cousins were still looking for her. He could not simply get rid of the body, he reasoned; he had to destroy it.

Hoisting Lindsay over his shoulder like a sack of cement, Heidnik carried her from the basement. Some time later the women heard what sounded like a power saw. They looked at each other and shivered.

Heidnik's dogs appeared, several hours after he had removed Lindsay's corpse, dragging a long white bone with chunks of red meat clinging to it. The women looked at the bone, and each thought the same thing: 'I wish I was close enough to grab the meat'.

A few days after Lindsay died, Heidnik bought a food processor and used it to grind up parts of her body. He even mixed the processed meat with dog food and fed it to his dogs and surviving captives. The rest of her body was put in white plastic bags and stacked neatly in the freezer compartment of his refrigerator.

The parts he could not grind — the head, hands,

feet and rib cage — he tried to destroy by cooking. However, that created a terrible stench, almost choking the women in the basement and so all-pervasive that it was noticed by many of Heidnik's neighbours.

Eventually, some residents alerted the police. But a rookie cop interviewed Heidnik and he convinced the officer that he had simply overcooked his dinner, so no further action was taken.

The smell hung around for days — polluting the air; permeating what little clothing the women captives had; and, most noticeably, virtually soaking into Heidnik himself. That night — for the first time since he had taken his first slave on 26 November — he did not go down to the cellar for sex. But for many days afterwards, when he resumed his sex-fix visits, he smelled so strongly of burning flesh that it was all the women could do to keep from gagging.

Heidnik did not know it yet, but his days were numbered; his grandiose plans for creating a basement baby factory were rapidly unravelling. Before they collapsed completely, however, his captives would undergo even more suffering and another one of them would die.

Between February and March, 1987, Heidnik inflicted horrendous punishments on his sex slave girls, including:

• Hanging each of the girls — one by one — to the eye-hook, with both their ankles cuffed and one arm above their heads. Then he would stuff a plastic bag in their mouths as a gag and secure it with duct tape wound around their heads. Finally, gripping them by the throat to keep them still, he would take a screwdriver and gouge in their ears, trying to damage their eardrums. 'He used three kinds of screwdrivers,' said Thomas later. 'Small, medium, and large. He twisted them in our ears until pus came out.'

• Showing any badly behaved slave Sandra Lindsay's head in a pot, as well as her ribs in a roasting pan and some of her other body parts in the freezer.

• Snipping off the plug end of an ordinary electrical extension cord and stripping the insulation to leave a bare wire, then plugging the other end into a socket. With current flowing through the wire, he would touch the bare end to the women's chains and laugh while they jumped and screamed.

Shortly after this, Deborah Dudley died when Heidnik electrocuted three of the girls who were crammed into the hole in the cellar floor. The wire went straight to her chain, so she took the heaviest jolt and died instantly.

At first Heidnik refused to believe that she had died. However, eventually he dragged her corpse out of the hole and laid it down in a far corner of the cellar.

'Aren't you glad it wasn't one of you?' Heidnik asked casually, before starting to make dogfood sandwiches for his slave girls.

He continued to have oral and vaginal sex with each of them with the intention of getting all or some of the remaining slave girls pregnant.

Shortly after the death of Dudley, Heidnik began to give Josefina Rivera considerably more freedom than his other slaves. Eventually, she managed to make her escape by convincing Heidnik that she would go out and find him a replacement for the recently departed Deborah Dudley. Instead, she went straight to the police. Just before midnight on 24 March, 1987, police detained Heidnik outside his house and took him in for questioning. He insisted he had done nothing wrong.

The following morning at 5am police, armed with a search warrant, crowbarred open the front door of the house after the keys provided by Heidnik proved useless. Once the door was opened, the police headed for the cellar.

White plastic shopping bags lay scattered around the room. A mattress lay in the middle of the room and on it were Lisa Thomas and Jacquelyn Askins, covered in blankets and snuggled up against each other for warmth. They were asleep.

When the women heard the commotion, they jolted awake and started screaming. They leapt to their feet, letting their blankets drop. Except for socks, they were both nude from the waist down. Both had shackles on their ankles and were connected to heavy chains.

'Are there any other women in the house?' asked one of the cops. 'Is there anyone here but you?'

Both women pointed to a pile of white plastic bags sitting on a board on the other side of the room.

'She's there,' said Thomas.

One of the cops remembered Rivera's early claims about dismemberment and picked up one of the plastic bags.

'Here?' he asked incredulously.

'No, under the board,' Thomas replied, 'She's in the hole.'

The cop pushed away the bags and slid the board

aside. Squatting at the bottom of a shallow pit was another woman, called Agnes Adams, who had been recently captured by Heidnik. She tried to stand up but lost her balance. The cops grabbed her arm and lifted her out. She was completely nude and shackled like the others and her hands were cuffed behind her back.

'We're free!' cried Thomas and Askins. They grabbed the two cops' hands and smothered them with kisses. 'We're saved!' they shrieked.

One of the cops took out a key and tried to unlock the handcuffs on Adams' hands. It did not fit. The other officer offered his cuff key and it worked. Then they removed her leg irons.

The women's ankles were covered with bruises and sores. Some wounds were fresh, but many had scabs. The police could not undo the nuts and sent word upstairs to fetch some bolt cutters. They also called for an ambulance and some extra hospital overalls for the women to wear.

The slave girls were skinny and looked like POWs. They were also starving hungry.

'He kept ice-cream in the freezer,' said Askins pointing to the box where Deborah Dudley's body had been kept until Heidnik found a place to dump it. 'Can we eat that?'

'I don't think you ought to have anything yet,' said one of the cops. 'Wait until the doctors check you over.' When their ankles had been unshackled, they were taken through the dining-room of the house. Heidnik had left some cookies on the table and the women grabbed these and wolfed them down.

As the women were whisked off to hospital, the

police fanned out through the house and began a painstaking search of the premises. They found a large stack of porno magazines, all of them featuring black women, on a closet shelf.

While one cop went upstairs, his colleague went into the kitchen. He looked at the stove and noticed an aluminium pot, its inside scorched and covered with a yellowish substance. In the open oven he saw a metal roasting pan that was charred on the inside and contained a piece of bone that looked suspiciously like a human rib. On the counter was a heavy-duty food processor, obviously used. The officer opened the freezer and saw a human forearm on the front shelf.

That was too much even for the hardened cop of twenty years' service. Feeling the bile rise in his throat, he ran outside and gulped in the fresh air, trying hard to keep from vomiting ...

On 2 July, 1988, just one hour and fifty-five minutes after they had begun their deliberations, the jury at the trial of Gary Heidnik pronounced the death sentence for each of the murders of Sandra Lindsay and Deborah Dudley.

Heidnik showed no emotion, but one of Lindsay's sisters sobbed quietly in the public gallery.

The killer's lawyer asked the judge to make sure Heidnik was kept in isolation at prison in case other inmates decided on some rough justice. The judge refused.

Outside the court the sister of Heidnik's murdered slave girl Deborah Dudley told reporters, 'My sister can rest in peace. We got what we wanted.'

On his way to prison in Pittsburgh, guards stopped

the bus to transfer other inmates and Heidnik was left alone momentarily with the other prisoners. As soon as the guards' backs were turned, they jumped him, and were still beating him when the guards rushed back to break it up. Such an incident, in prison slang, is called 'a tuning up'.

But it was nothing compared with being put in a hole in the ground. No one beat him with shovel handles. No one gouged in his ears with screwdrivers. No one made him eat human body parts or dog food. It is perhaps appropriate that the punishment Heidnik was sentenced to receive actually fitted the crime he committed. He was to be electrocuted — the same way that his second victim, Deborah Dudley, died …

4

Fear and Loathing in Shimodate

'Servitude debases men to the point where they end up liking it.'

Reflections And Maxims, Vauvenargues, 1746

Shimodate, near Tokyo, Japan, Summer 1991.

The town, made up mainly of a soulless grid of convenience stores and amusement arcades, is located on the outer reaches of the Tokyo commuter belt. Its residents comprise prosperous farmers, bored bureaucrats and corporate workers.

However, beneath this dull veneer, prostitution thrives. Bars and 'love hotels' run by Japanese gangsters, the Yakuza, clog the backstreets, their neon-lit signs flickering garishly. In dark alleys, scantily clad women beckon men for sex. On the main street, drunks wander from club to club.

Just a few months earlier, Goong, Roon and Noi — all in their mid-twenties — were living in Thailand's rural north. Goong, a lively, oval-faced woman, was supporting her elderly parents on a meagre hospital cleaner's salary. Roon, a svelte divorcee with a seven-year-old daughter, was juggling three part-time jobs. Noi, a frail 25-year-old, was working twelve-hour shifts in a local sweatshop. None could resist when they were approached by friendly recruiters offering substantial wages as waitresses or factory workers in Japan.

Goong was the first to realise she had been horribly duped. On arrival in Shimodate, she was met by a broker who promptly 'sold' her for two million yen (£13,000) to a woman called Lek, a 28-year-old Thai with cropped hair and sullen features, who ran a prostitution racket in league with the Yakuza. Roon and Noi later met with the same fate.

Within hours of landing in Japan, Lek told them how the system worked: the women now owed her 3.5 million yen (£22,000) each to cover their purchase price and her own profit, and they would have to sell their bodies to pay her back.

Lek took their passports, cash and return plane tickets. 'If you escape, I'll turn the world upside down to find you,' she warned. 'If I find you, I'll kill you. If I don't, I'll send someone to kill your parents.'

Goong, Roon and Noi were then taken to Lek's apartment in Shimodate. They were terrified, bewildered and very homesick, but they had no choice. Within hours, Lek had introduced them to other Thai slave girls whom she 'owned' and they were told to start work in a local bar, called the Mimi. Their jobs were to pour drinks and clap at the customers' karaoke efforts. But their real duties were soon made clear: to provide sex for men looking for relief from the tedium of their lives in the Tokyo suburbs.

The three women were stunned. None of them had ever done such 'work' before. 'Prostitution was against everything I believed in,' Goong later recalled, 'I couldn't accept it. My misery was too overwhelming to describe.'

Lek had an arrangement with the Mimi bar whereby the Thai women would work on the premises for nothing and, in return, the bar would serve as a front for her shameless pimping.

Goong, Roon and Noi were expected to have sex with at least three men every night and they were not allowed any time off, even when they were sick.

Goong later explained, 'The customers often liked to do things they would never do with their wives.' That included regular demands for fellatio, which all three of the women particularly hated.

One time, Goong refused to have oral sex with a man because of his poor hygiene. When he complained to Lek, she dragged Goong from the room in her apartment where they were having sex and beat her. Goong was later convinced that Lek got a sexual kick from hitting her.

Lek further punished Goong by telling all prospective clients that she gave 'excellent blow-jobs'.

The other girls did not fare any better. Noi was almost drowned by a customer after she refused to let him perform anal sex on her. He ducked her head repeatedly in a hot bath-tub and then forced her on to her knees ...

All three slave girls were regularly spat on, punched and burned with cigarettes. And some clients insisted on using handcuffs and other restraints during sex. 'The men treated us like animals,' explained Roon.

Yet a police station stood just 300 yards from the apartment block where Lek was overseeing her brutal regime. However, the women could not go there for help because many of the local police were customers and Yoko Sasaki — the tough female owner of the Mimi Bar — warned them that a simple pay-off to the police by the Yakuza would ensure that any allegations would be reported directly back to Lek.

'In any case, the police would arrest you for being illegal immigrants,' warned Lek. The isolation of the slave girls was complete.

They spoke no Japanese and were never allowed out alone. They could write to their families, but Lek censored all letters. She also pocketed every yen of the women's salary to repay their 'debt', and devised a strict system of fines to ensure that their tab never reached zero.

The cost of everything — from their food to their frayed second-hand dresses — was billed to them. If three days passed without a customer, they were fined 26,000 yen (£160). Lek said men preferred skinny girls and allowed them to eat only two meals a day. They often felt dizzy with hunger.

As the months slowly passed, the three slave girls began to doubt that they would ever escape alive. Lek issued daily death-threats, boasting that she knew their addresses in Thailand and had the right connections to keep her word.

'Even if we had paid off our debts, she would never have released us alive,' says Roon today. 'We knew too much about her.' In sheer desperation, Goong, Roon and Noi slowly decided they had no choice: they would have to strike first.

At 5am on a crisp autumn day in September, 1991, Roon was woken by Goong pulling at her arm. 'I can't stand it anymore,' she whispered. 'We have to do it now.' Roon crawled out of bed well aware that only Lek and her two slave girl companions were in the apartment that night. Goong went to fetch Noi. The three talked in whispers until they all agreed that Lek had to be killed. They headed for the kitchen, where the only potential weapons were an eight-centimetre knife, a bottle of sake and a garden trowel. Goong handed the knife to Roon in silence. Roon's hands shook so much that she gave it back. For a few endless seconds, the three passed the knife between them until Noi, the youngest and seemingly most timid, finally accepted it.

As dawn broke, the three women crept to Lek's bedside. She was sleeping curled up on her side, making a clean hit difficult. Goong put her hands together and prayed, 'If Lek's life is to end tonight, please God, let her turn over.'

To Goong's amazement, Lek instantly complied.

Neither Roon, Goong or Noi can recall who actually struck first.

'I saw Noi raise the knife and I closed my eyes,' recalls Roon. 'Lek screamed. Then I heard the sound of

a bottle shattering and the smell of sake filled the room.'
Lek began to thrash wildly Goong shouted for Roon to
hold the wounded woman's legs to stop them moving.
There was blood and broken glass everywhere.

A few minutes later, Lek fell still — unconscious or
dead — the slave girls did not know. Goong told Roon
to help her remove Lek's gold jewellery, while Noi
searched for the waist pouch where they thought Lek
kept their passports. Noi grabbed Lek's locked red
handbag in case their documents were in there.

The three women then made off across the rice
paddy in front of the apartment complex. At the other
side, they hailed a taxi and gestured for the driver to take
them to a hotel. Once inside their room, Goong washed
the bloody jewellery. This was to be their plane ticket
home, together with 200,000 yen (£1,300) in bar tips
that they had saved by sewing the money into their
dresses.

Roon forced open Lek's locked red handbag to see
if their passports were inside, while Noi unzipped the
waist pouch. When the contents of both bags tumbled
out, the three were stupefied. The handbag contained a
mountain of gold jewellery, the pouch nearly seven
million yen (£43,000).

Back at Lek's place, one of her other slave girls
discovered her corpse and called the police. By the time
investigators arrived, bar-keeper Yoko Sasaki and her
Yakuza gangster husband were there to enlighten police
about what might have happened. They claimed the
three women were 'cold-hearted whores' who had a
grudge against Lek.

Detectives soon tracked down the three runaway

slave girls at their hotel by using the taxi driver's logbook. They immediately confessed to the killing but insisted they had only thought about taking the money after Lek had been stabbed.

'We only wanted to escape,' said Roon. But the police were highly suspicious and, to add to the confusion, none of the women spoke Japanese, so two Thai housewives had to be recruited to act as interpreters.

Nine hours later, the slave girls were presented with statements written in Japanese and asked to sign them. 'I thought I would get home sooner if we signed,' said Noi later.

At this stage the women did not even have lawyers. Three weeks after the stabbing, Goong, Roon and Noi were charged with murder in the course of a robbery. The authorities cited their 'signed confessions' as justification for the charge.

The case aroused a lot of controversy in Japan because it was the first time that victims of the flesh trade had actually killed to escape. Young female lawyer Chinami Kajo took on the case and immediately insisted, 'It was clear that the women's circumstances had been completely ignored by the police. They didn't want to admit that the problem of sex trafficking was involved because then they'd have to take action against the pimps and brothel owners. Most police don't want to get their hands dirty fighting prostitution rackets.'

Kajo and her team of five lawyers decided to fight for a complete acquittal on the grounds of self-defence. The odds against them were astronomical — in Japan's non-jury legal system, a staggering 99.4 per cent of criminal cases are won outright by the prosecution, mostly on the basis of signed confessions. 'The confession is the highest form of evidence here,' explained one Japanese legal expert. 'When the prosecution bases its case on such evidence, the judges rarely dispute it.'

When the slave girls' trial began in December, 1991, the lawyers' first task was to try to discredit Goong, Roon and Noi's supposed confessions. They claimed that untrained interpreters had been unable to translate the difference between 'murder and theft' and 'murder in the course of robbery', so the women had no idea what they were confessing to.

Another uphill task was for the defence to prove that Goong, Roon and Noi had been forced into a life of sexual slavery. 'We had to show that they had fallen prey to international slave traders,' explained Kajo. 'But we had no witnesses — it was impossible to find the recruiters and brokers responsible.'

Even more surprising was that even if they had found the perpetrators, it would have been virtually impossible to prosecute them because of Japan's draconian attitude towards slavery. There are no laws relating to the trafficking of women into Japan, only a nineteenth-century statute which prohibits the sale of Japanese women abroad.

The defence team did have one woman — bar owner Yoko Sasaki — whom they accused of flagrantly abetting prostitution. But she was not too worried because she had landed the plum role of star prosecution witness.

The victim, Lek, was herself proving to be a real mystery. After her death it took the police sixty-one days to identify her. She had first come to Japan in 1983 and had been deported once, probably as a result of the same prostitution activities she had since forced on others. All that was left of her was an accounts book in which she had logged her employees' debts and her human purchases. Between 15 January 1990 and her death, she had bought twenty-eight women for 56 million yen (£300,000).

Kajo and her team resorted to using experts who could testify about the sex slave-trafficking industry between Thailand and Japan. One of them — Buddhist temple chief priest Akimichi Sugiura — told the court, 'Recruiters in Thailand target rural areas to find naive women. They are the first link in the chain, and are often local people or most insidious of all, women who were once victims of forced prostitution themselves. They pass on their female prey to members of organised crime syndicates.'

Sugiura believes the flesh trade between Japan and Thailand is worth up to £600 million a year. Most of the women are brought to non-urban areas of Japan where demand is highest and law enforcement less rigid. In Ibaraki alone — the region including the town of Shirnodate — there are some 4,000 Thai female sex slaves working in up to 400 prostitution bars.

Throughout Japan, there are believed to be 90,000 such women from Thailand and other south-east Asian countries such as the Philippines and Malaysia.

Although it was impossible to prove whether Lek would ever have carried out her threat to murder Goong, Roon and Noi, their defence lawyers argued that their fears were not unfounded. For a total of forty-three south-east Asian women have died in prostitution-related killings in Japan since 1991. And at the very same time as the Shimodate trial, a Thai pimp was prosecuted in a nearby city for hiring a hit-man to murder two slave girl prostitutes who had escaped without paying off their debts. The hit-man had already been convicted.

But at the trial of Goong, Roon and Noi, prosecutors continued to insist that claims that the three slaves had acted in self-defence were completely bogus. Star prosecution witness, bar-keeper Yoko Sasaki, continued to run her own prostitution/slave racket throughout the trial — a fact the prosecution simply overlooked. Sasaki told the court that Lek had behaved like a mother to the three women. She actually claimed the slave girls only ever worked as bar hostesses and never as prostitutes.

In his closing argument, the prosecutor proposed that Goong, Roon and Noi be sentenced to life imprisonment, as a deterrent to 'similar crimes by foreigners'. He did not ask for the death penalty, but the news was still a blow.

At the final hearing in March, 1995, the three women pleaded for understanding. 'I'm truly sorry we killed,' said Goong, 'I am quietly seeking forgiveness every day.'

Roon promised never to commit such a crime again. 'I have decided to become a nun when I return to Thailand,' she told the court. A distraught Noi could only whisper, 'I'm sorry.'

On the day of the verdict — 23 May, 1995 — supporters of the three women camped outside the provincial courthouse. Sympathy for their plight had gathered momentum, particularly because two virtually identical killings had occurred almost a year after the Shimodate murder.

Six Thai women had killed a Taiwanese brothel keeper in Tokyo during an escape attempt; later that year, five Thai women stabbed their Singaporean boss to death. The fact that there was no 'robbery' involved in either of those other cases raised the possibility in a few minds that maybe Goong, Roon and Noi had been telling the truth about their slavery.

The three runaway sex slaves could barely muster a smile as they were led into the tiny courtroom to hear their fate. They were dressed in jeans, white T-shirts and plastic prison slippers. They stood facing the three judges as the verdict was read out: they were declared guilty of murder in the course of robbery and sentenced to ten years' imprisonment each. Goong and Noi began to cry. Roon remained expressionless.

The judge then explained the verdict. A call for life sentences had been rejected because, significantly, the women were deemed to have been under 'mental and physical strain'. But the claims of self-defence were also disregarded: the women, he said, had conspired to rob Lek and killed her in a 'brutal manner'. Kajo immediately announced plans to appeal.

The three women were inconsolable. 'All the energy we've put into trying to tell the truth has been wasted,' explained Goong. 'Why don't they believe us?' Noi, too, was 'shocked and upset'. Roon had other things on her mind. 'When will I see my daughter?' she pondered miserably.

Strangely, however, the trial had some positive

results. In showing the terrible extremes to which Goong, Roon and Noi had been driven, more people were shocked into joining the fight against sex trafficking and slavery. 'Now more groups and individuals realise that such slavery still exists here and must be stopped,' says lawyer Chinami Kajo. She points to the need for stricter laws against the flesh trade, and to shift the current focus of punishment from the prostitutes to the pimps. 'There is no excuse for police inaction now.'

Goong, Roon and Noi are also aware that their case is a cautionary tale. 'We want to publicise our experience as much as possible,' says Goong from prison, 'to prevent other women from falling into the same trap.'

5

A Twisted Mind

'The moment the slave resolves that he will no longer be a slave, his fetters fall. He frees himself and shows the way for others. Freedom and slavery are mental states.'

Mohandas Karamchand Gandhi, 1949

Sao Joao De Loure, Portugal, June, 1990.

Susanna's face had an affinity with light. Her skin was the colour of pale chocolate and her dark hair still glistened despite the dreadful conditions she lived in. But it was the brown of her eyes, like jewels on velvet under a showcase spotlight, that were her most defiant feature. Even during the most terrible of physical attacks, those eyes refused to show fear. Their beam was unwavering, never betraying any of the terror that she must have felt when she suffered yet another beating.

Jorge Ferreira, looking into those eyes, was

infuriated by their strength. For within his blubbery body lay a twisted mind. A mind warped by time. A mind that wanted Susanna all to himself. He was determined to take what he required from her — whenever he felt like it. How dearly the innocent Susanna would have to pay.

'I'm so hungry, senor. Please, there must be something to eat.' As she looked up at him, her chains clanked. Ferreira looked down at her with disgust and contempt.

'Shut up, nigger.'

'But please, senor. Anything.'

Ferreira smirked.

'Anything?'

'Yes. Please ... '

He picked up a lump of cow dung from the floor of the barn and squeezed it in his huge hand.

'Try this, nigger.'

Moments later, wretched Susanna gagged as Ferreira tried to ram the stinking cow dung down her throat. He pinched her nose and forced some of it into her mouth.

'Never ask me for food again.'

Ferreira gave her a kick in the kidneys for good measure and marched out of the barn that stood 300 yards from his vast mansion in the remote village of Sao Joao de Loure, 160 miles north of the Portuguese capital of Lisbon.

Another day in the tortured life of Susanna dos Santos had come to an end. The few hours of sleep she got every night in that draughty outhouse were a welcome relief from the harsh reality of her situation.

Susanna and her friend Emilia's suffering had begun sixteen years earlier in the Angolan jungle where Ferreira had settled during the fifties when the Portuguese were still very much in command of this colony.

Ferreira made a small fortune from trading cattle, charcoal and groceries at a bush outpost. He later boasted to one reporter, 'I had 3,000 blacks working for me then.' He was proud of his ability to get the locals to work and ran his life very much along the lines of those brutal slave masters in the deep south of the United States in the mid-1800s.

Ferreira was renowned for having a whole harem of black slave girls in those days. They would be expected to perform any duty he required at the click of his fingers. He had an extensive collection of firearms and did not hesitate to use them if any of his workers disobeyed his orders.

He would frequently tell friends that he wanted to raise his own slave girls 'so that they do absolutely everything I want without question. It's better to catch them young and then mould them into precisely what one wants.'

Stories of Ferreira's brutal treatment of his slaves were commonplace. There were even rumours that he had a couple of 'favourites' whom he kept shackled in a barn near his huge mansion. Many people suspected that the bulky entrepreneur used and abused them whenever it took his fancy.

So it was not really very surprising that, when Ferreira heard of two unwanted babies in the local village, he bought them for a pittance from their families. His sole intention was to bring them up as his personal slave girls. Ferreira's power was such within that backward community that no one would have dared question his actions.

Whenever any of the numerous other colonists questioned Ferreira's actions, he told them, 'No one else would have cared for them. They would have been dead within a year if I hadn't taken them on.'

At least at the beginning he seemed to treat the two girls reasonably. However, the first thing he did was strip them both of their local native names and re-christen them Susanna and Emilia.

'They're my property now and I'll call them whatever I like,' Ferreira told one nosy neighbour in Angola.

For the following few years, Susanna and Emilia were trained by Ferreira for their eventual duties as fully fledged slave girls. He wanted to ensure that they were obedient in every quarter. No task would be too much for them — he would make sure of that.

When Angola gained its independence from Portugal in 1975, Ferreira somehow managed to smuggle the two girls back with him to Portugal, even though they had no passports.

Once home in the village of Sao Joao de Loure, Ferreira set the girls to work and forced them to live in a draughty outhouse while he, his wife and three daughters lived in relative luxury in the main farmhouse. While Ferreira's children attended the local school, his young girl slaves were put to work each day from dawn until late at night, even though they were both still under the age of ten at the time.

At night, Susanna and Emilia were chained up on the straw-strewn floor of the barn to prevent their escape. They were also kept on starvation rations that consisted of leftovers tipped into a bowl, which they both ate with their hands.

There were no toilet facilities in the outhouse, so the girls would urinate and defecate like animals and occasionally one of Ferreira's farm workers would rake it all up.

Many of the other workers on the farm were aware of the girls' plight, but they did nothing for fear they would lose their jobs or face a violent backlash from heavyweight Ferreira if they dared stand up to his habitual bullying.

Frequently, the slave girls would be given no food at all. On other occasions they would be taken out into the fields that surrounded the farm and told to eat animal fodder. When the girls complained, Ferreria threatened to make them eat cow dung.

But when the girls reached their early teens, Ferreira's demands became more extreme. Sometimes he would appear in the barn, drunk, unzip his pants and insist they each perform oral sex on him. Then he would try to have sex with one or both of the girls, but usually he gave up because he was so drunk.

At night the girls were so cold that they would snuggle up to each other to keep warm. Once, Ferreira stumbled into the outhouse and tried to get them to perform sexual acts on each other. The poor, innocent slave girls had no idea that gay love existed, let alone how to perform it in front of their master.

If ever either of the girls objected to his sexual

advances, Ferreira would take out his favourite bullwhip, force the offending girl to pull down her tattered trousers and whip her on her bare behind. Then he would frequently commit some kind of sex act to satisfy the obvious excitement he felt at beating them.

Ferreira's other favourite instruments of torture included a truncheon and a stave. Often he would punish the girls for no apparent reason other than that he gained some perverted delight from inflicting pain on them.

Worst still were the living conditions. As the girls grew into their teens they continued to sleep on old straw, often soaked with urine and virtually every night one or other of them would be bitten by one of the dozens of rats which also lived in the barn. Susanna bears the scars from the beatings and rat bites to this day.

Both girls were forbidden to talk to the townspeople of Sao Joao de Loure, but they were sometimes sent out shopping. Fatima Abreu, a hairdresser, said later that their plight was obvious to everyone because of the cuts, bruises and welts disfiguring their faces.

'It was a local scandal,' she said. 'But Ferreira was such a violent figure that people were afraid to offer the girls shelter.'

In 1985, Emilia was claimed by her father, a Portuguese man who had known Ferreira in Angola. He took her to another village and tried to help her start a new life. But Emilia could not escape the nightmarish memories of those awful years at the hands of Ferreira and she committed suicide just a few months after her 'escape' from that horrendous life of slavery. She had complained to her family about constant nightmares and she desperately missed Susanna who had been her only friend in the world for virtually her entire life. In the end, she felt she just could not carry on.

Unaware of what had happened to her only friend, Susanna had no choice but to stay with Ferreira. She was illiterate, unable to wash properly and completely unprepared for the outside world. She knew that Ferreira was a bad man, but she did not know where to go for refuge.

However, as she reached her late teens, Susanna started repeatedly to question her situation. She was curious about life and she determined that one day she would pick her moment and get away from evil Ferreira. Meanwhile, her overweight master started to force himself upon her more and more regularly.

It was not until a few years later that she finally plucked up the courage to flee his property and plead for sanctuary at the house of local couple, hairdresser Fatima and her husband, Antonio Abreu.

At first, Susanna was too frightened to report her plight to the authorities. She feared that Ferreira would come after her and hunt her down in the way he had always threatened he would if she ever ran away. Eventually the Abreus persuaded Susanna to take her story to the police, who finally charged Ferreira under a law prohibiting slavery.

'When Susanna came here she was about eighteen years old, but she had never been toilet-trained and only knew how to eat with her hands. She was very traumatised psychologically,' said Fatima Abreu.

The Susanna of today is a very different person, even though her new home is just 200 metres away from her one time 'owner', Ferreira. She often sees the fearsome farmer outside his house but has not exchanged a word with him since her escape.

Susanna has now married and is brimming with hope and confidence for the future. She secured her identity documents, which she needed to get married, through the Angolan embassy in Lisbon.

'I remember that my original African name was Kiumbi,' she says. 'Ferreira invented the name Susanna, but for the thirteen years I was with him I was only called "nigger" and never addressed by any name at all.' As for Ferreira, a corpulent man in his late sixties, he spends most of his time sitting on his porch, brooding over what he sees as the injustice of the case against him.

Cursing the law and the press, he has insisted he did nothing wrong, though he openly admitted he had beaten Susanna on occasions as 'punishment for stealing fruit from the neighbours'.

He added, 'How could they could they try an old man like me? I spent a fortune bringing up those girls. I gave them everything and this is how they reward me.' Ferreira was eventually found guilty of enslaving Susanna and her friend Emilia and sentenced to three years in prison.

6

Help Me Please!

'Whatever happens to them is happening inside the house, and what goes on inside the house is personal. In Kuwait, homes are traditionally and constitutionally sacred places.'

Ghnim al-Najjar, Kuwaiti human rights activist

Kuwait City, Kuwait, 4 October, 1991.

Kuwaitis are surely among the most privileged and pampered people in history. With their vast oil wealth, they simply hire people to do almost all their work.

Before the invasion by Iraq on 2 August, 1990, eighty per cent of the labour force was non-Kuwaiti, and there were 200,000 non-Kuwaiti servants in the country. At that time, every family had five or six servants but after the invasion, the Kuwaitis decided for security reasons to reduce the number of foreigners in the country. Consequently, in October, 1991, the Minister of the Interior issued regulations limiting the number of servants a family could employ: a family of five could have only two; a family larger than that could have four. Many Kuwaitis found the restrictions too harsh, however, and within a week the law was amended to allow a family to pay an annual fee if they wanted more servants.

So it was that Jenny Casanova from the Philippines came to be employed as a slave maid in Kuwait.

'Where are the children's shoes. WHERE?'

The mistress of the house was once again screaming at Jenny Casanova, 'I told you to put them in the cupboard. Where are they?'

Jenny looked nervously at her mistress. She had been through this so many times before that she knew what was probably going to come next.

'I try to find them. I try,' she pleaded with the woman.

Jenny moved out of the children's room to see if the shoes were in a cupboard in the hallway, but she heard the woman follow her.

'You stupid bitch! You lose everything!'

'But the children are always leaving them around the house,' Jenny replied. It was a careless response in the circumstances and she knew what would follow even before she had finished uttering her defiant reply.

The first punch connected with her lower abdomen. It was her mistress's favourite first 'hit'. She followed it up with a series of stinging slaps to the face. Jenny tried to cover her face with her hands to prevent the scratching she had suffered from her mistress's blood-red fingernails in the past.

But the woman grabbed Jenny's wrist and pulled her hand down before smacking her hard across the cheeks.

'Please. Stop,' pleaded Jenny.

But it was to no avail. This was only the beginning.

Her mistress continued yelling, 'You're useless. What do I pay you all this money for? You can't even find the children's shoes.'

'All this money' consisted of £110 a month. Less than a third of the minimum wage in oil-rich Kuwait. Just then, the beating stopped and the woman moved determinedly towards a cupboard further down the hall. Jenny slumped against the wall, relieved that her latest beating seemed to be over. She turned and headed back to the children's room.

Suddenly, she heard a whistling sound, then moments later a stinging sensation on her backside.

'You need to be taught a lesson, girl,' her mistress screamed as she started whacking her slave girl with a cane.

The stick came down on Jenny with such force that it made her crouch in a corner of the hallway. Unfortunately, this simply presented the women with an even easier target. She began thrashing Jenny across her backside and the backs of her thighs. What seemed like dozens of strokes followed.

As Jenny crouched on the tiled floor, trying to roll herself into a ball to avoid the worst of the attack, her skirt rode up, exposing more flesh to her mistress. This seemed to enrage her still further and the beating became even more intense.

'I will teach you to be insolent. How dare you answer me back. Only speak when spoken to. Do you understand?'

Jenny tried to nod her head in the hope that it might persuade her mistress to stop the thrashing. Eventually she halted proceedings because she seemed to be growing bored with inflicting that particular form of punishment.

'Don't move. Stay here,' screamed her mistress.

Jenny shivered with fear as she watched her mistress go back to the cupboard where she had got the cane a few minutes earlier.

This time she emerged with a vacuum-cleaner hose. As Jenny tried to scramble to her feet, the first blow knocked her back down to the floor. Jenny was hit at least a dozen more times before the mistress of the house decided she had made her point. The young slave was lying crumpled up on the floor, too scared to move in case it provoked yet another attack.

'Get up,' said the mistress. 'Get up — NOW!'

Jenny looked up at the angry, twisted face of her employer and tried to use the wall to support herself as she attempted to stand up.

'Get your dirty hands off my clean walls!'

Jenny fell back against the wall. She could not see properly through her tear-filled eyes and the pain searing through the lower half of her body was excruciating.

'I'll be back in five minutes and I expect you to have cleaned out the children's rooms,' barked her mistress.

Another day in the household from hell had begun

for domestic slave girl Jenny Casanova.

It all seemed a million miles away from the brightly coloured streets of Manila, in the Philippines, where pretty dark-haired Jenny had lived until a year earlier.

With three daughters all under the age of ten and no job, 30-year-old Jenny had actively sought work in Kuwait 'for the future of my children'.

Her first move was to join an employment agency that promised to place women in jobs in the wealthy Middle East for the equivalent of a £300 fee.

Jenny was over the moon when the agency announced that they had found her a family to work for in Kuwait City. Little did she realise that she was about to begin a long-term nightmare.

On arrival at the impressive detached house in an immaculate, wealthy suburb, Jenny actually believed that she would be reasonably happy. And in any case, her salary would help pay for her children's upkeep back in Manila and that was all that really mattered.

The master of the house was a civil servant who worked long hours, but his wife and their four children seemed the epitome of domestic family bliss when Jenny arrived.

She definitely felt a slight coldness towards her from all the family members, but she took that to be shyness and presumed they would all get on in the end. But within hours of arriving, she was told that her salary would be withheld for at least the first two months to recover part of what the master of the house had paid to a Kuwaiti recruitment agency. Jenny was a little disturbed by this but decided to get down to work on the basis that once that initial period was completed she could then send all her wages back to her needy family in Manila.

Jenny rose at 5.30am every morning to clean the house before the family woke. Her room was a tiny cubicle with a mattress on the floor. Over the first few days, the mistress laid down some bizarre ground rules. 'You must only rest in your room when your duties are over,' she barked.

A few days later, Jenny noticed that the mistress got very angry when she caught her husband talking to Jenny in the hallway.

'You talk to me only. Do you understand?'

Jenny nodded nervously. It soon became apparent that no one in that family was even going to give her the time of day. The family dog got more attention than she did.

Within a few weeks, her life was governed by a gruelling routine — rising before dawn and working until at least midnight every day of the week. She had to do all the cooking and cleaning and take care of four children aged fifteen, fourteen, twelve and six.

One day Jenny — a strict Catholic — asked her mistress if she could go to church.

'Filipinos don't go outside. Ever,' came the reply. Jenny heard the dangerous tension in her mistress's voice. Shortly after that, she received the first of the regular beatings that became a terrifying feature of life inside that house.

By the time of that dreadful thrashing inflicted because she could not find the children's shoes, Jenny had reached the end of her tether.

As she crawled into the bathroom to try to tend to

her wounds, she felt a wave of despair overcome her. She was trapped in a strange land without enough money to get home, in a house dominated by a sadistic employer who had threatened her with death if she dared to try to escape.

Intriguingly, the mistress obviously sensed that Jenny was contemplating escape because later that same day, she insisted that Jenny went with her to visit a sick relative. Clearly, she feared that Jenny might run away if left alone in the house.

'You have to leave before she kills you,' one of the maids at that relative's house told Jenny as the two women sat down in the servants' quarters for a cup of tea, while their mistresses talked upstairs.

Ironically, it was thanks to her employer taking her to that other house that she found the courage to leave. The other maid had been so shocked to hear about the beatings and non-stop verbal abuse that she told Jenny to leave immediately, before she returned to the house and found herself trapped with nowhere to go.

Pointing to the driveway outside the house, the other maid said, 'Walk slowly to the gate, then run.'

She gave Jenny a dinar and hugged her.

'You have to do it.'

Jenny left the house and hailed a taxi which took her to the Philippine Embassy in the city. There she found more than two hundred other Filipino maids who had all fled their employers in Kuwait City. The abuse of domestic staff was clearly a serious problem.

The reasons for this widespread mistreatment of maids in Kuwait and elsewhere can be attributed partly to cultural traditions and values.

'First, it is because they are women, and women are mistreated generally in Kuwait,' explains Eman al-Bedah, a Kuwaiti human-rights activist. 'Second, because they are maids. They are lower class and people exercise their power over them.'

Bedah herself employs two Sri Lankan maids but she allows them to attend regular religious services and they may receive phonecalls and have visits from friends. She is the exception.

'Our neighbours say we are spoiling them,' says Bedah.

Much of the reporting of mistreatment in recent years has focused on rape and sexual abuse by men. However, the women responsible for supervising the slave maids and who have contact with them during the day are guilty of the worst atrocities.

'Many of them are treating their maids in the same way their husbands treat them,' says Bedah.

The status of women in Kuwait is marked by contradictions. Their political rights are severely restricted — they do not even have the right to vote — but the popular Western image of the veiled Arab woman, docile and subservient to her husband, does not apply in Kuwait. They do go out alone and they are allowed to wear western clothes.

However, the Asian maids in Kuwait suffer from more than just being women in a male-dominated society. They are foreigners in an extremely closed and xenophobic society. No one is automatically entitled to citizenship; they must prove that their family has lived there since before 1920.

That leaves tens of thousands of essentially stateless people, many of whom were born in Kuwait and have lived their entire lives in the country, and whose fathers and grandfathers were born there, but who are not actual Kuwaiti citizens. Even other Arabs are considered inferior by the Kuwaitis, and the maids, being Asians, are at the bottom of the pile.

'People don't see it as a problem; they don't think that many are mistreated,' says Ghanim al-Najjar, a prominent human-rights activist with a strictly pro-government stance.

He even insists, 'We have a lot of maids in this country, and abuse and mistreatment are not very common.'

As for the failure of the Kuwaiti government to protect the maids, he says, 'Whatever happens to the maids is happening inside the house, and what goes on inside the house is personal. In Kuwait, homes are traditionally and constitutionally sacred places.' In other words, it is not the business of the State to regulate anything that happens in the home.

He also said, 'It's very hard to know what really happens. If a maid says she's been beaten or neglected, how on earth can you prove that?'

Back in the Philippine Embassy in Kuwait City, Jenny Casanova nursed a black, blue and yellow left eye — a direct result of that final beating from her mistress — as well as a large bruise on her upper right arm and bruises on her left calf and thigh.

Then, to her horror, she saw her mistress's husband being shown into an office next to the room where she was seated with dozens of other abused maids.

Jenny rushed to the embassy secretary sitting nearby.

'What's he doing here? He's not taking me back. Never.'

It then transpired that her former employer had come to the embassy to try to persuade Jenny to go to the employment agency that had brought her to Kuwait, so he could reclaim the money he had paid for her.

'I want my passport back first,' demanded Jenny, safe in the knowledge that neither he nor his wife could do anything to harm her while she remained in the embassy.

The man pleaded with Jenny to accompany him to the recruitment agency.

'You have to help me. I want my money back.'

But Jenny was in no mood to be helpful to the husband of the woman who had sadistically beaten her for months.

'I just want my passport.'

It was a stalemate and neither party could win. Then, in an extraordinary outburst, the man insisted that Jenny had actually been the one hitting his wife. 'But my wife hit her back She got what she deserved,' he claimed. In the end, he stormed out of the embassy, crossed the street and got into a gold-coloured Cadillac.

Jenny Casanova was just one of tens of thousands of young Asian women who have come to Kuwait to find work and escape the poverty back at home.

The Kuwaiti Government reckons there are 71,000 domestic servants from Asia, including 30,000 from India, 25,000 from the Philippines, 11,000 from

Bangladesh and 5,000 from Sri Lanka. Almost none of them speak Arabic, and the language barrier frequently results in problems between employer and employee. Many of the maids are recruited by unscrupulous agencies which take their money without telling them what lies ahead, or even, in some cases, where they are going.

In Kuwait and throughout the Persian Gulf states these women are taken advantage of by their employers: they are forced to work long hours for low pay, and are often virtually enslaved. They find that they have no place to go for protection. The Kuwaiti Government offers them next to nothing, and their own embassies in Kuwait help them only grudgingly.

Many employers do not appreciate the situation because they consider it a matter of principle not to allow the slave maids to leave, as they have paid substantial fees to agencies to get them in the first place.

The police station in the Dasma district of Kuwait City is a ramshackle, three-storey building, in which policemen in white robes lounge around on sagging vinyl-covered couches.

The Dasma police station has become a sort of informal complaint-resolution centre for runaway slave maids. Between five and six o'clock most evenings, buses arrive from the embassies with maids who have fled the homes of employers.

Most of the women hope that the police can persuade their employers to return their passport, and maybe even the money for a ticket home.

Virtually all of them claim to have been beaten and

treated like slaves. But some of them even insisted they had been beaten by the woman who ran one particular recruitment agency after their employers had taken them back, complaining that the maids did not work hard enough.

The Kuwaiti Government recently passed regulations to license the recruitment agencies, but these regulations are unlikely to be enforced since the agencies are owned by Kuwaitis. And even though Kuwait does have laws against assault, they have never been enforced when a maid has been attacked by her employer.

Officials in the Ministry of the Interior — which has responsibility for maids — cannot provide any documentation to prove that any man has ever been prosecuted for the rape of a maid, or that a woman has been prosecuted for beating a maid. Philippine and Sri Lankan diplomats claim that they are not aware of any criminal prosecutions of employers for assaults on maids. It seems unlikely that the situation will change until the Kuwaitis themselves are willing to acknowledge the seriousness of the problem.

As if to prove that point, in 1993 Kuwait offered to fly home many of the abused slave/servants — at more than twice the regular airfare. The Government said the additional costs were to provide Kuwaiti employers with a 'reimbursement fee'.

'We cannot afford this. We are stuck,' said Yolanda Rodriguez, housemother to many of the women who have taken refuge at the Philippine Embassy.

'Our life is worth nothing to the Kuwaitis,' said another abused servant, Marife Venzon.

7

The Root of all Evil

'All punishment is mischief.
All punishment in itself is evil.'

Jeremy Bentham, 1789

Tijuana, Mexico, Summer, 1985.

Cynthia Montano wondered what the hell she was doing, kerb-crawling around the seediest part of this chaotic border town. But her employer, Santee Kimes, had been most insistent that she wanted two more girls immediately and Cynthia knew it was more than her job was worth not to carry out her wishes.

The rental car was inconspicuous, despite the California plates, because Tijuana was literally swarming with visitors who had popped across the border for a taste of the cheap local liquor and women.

As Cynthia turned down a sidestreet, she spotted two young girls who looked perfect. 'Make sure they don't wear make-up or jewellery,' Santee Kimes had told her before she set off from the Kimes' impressive mansion in La Jolla, California, just forty miles from the border with Mexico.

'And they have to be very subservient,' were Kimes' last words as Cynthia drove off in her rental Ford. Now, just two hours later, she seemed to have found exactly what her mistress required.

Cynthia slowed the car down and the electric window descended quietly.

'Hola. Com esta?'

The two girls looked up, smiling. They could not have been much more than fourteen or fifteen years old. Cynthia got out of the car and started her own gentle interrogation of the two prospective slaves. But one of the girls seemed uneasy. She told Cynthia that her parents would never let her just leave town for a job in California. Cynthia's heart sunk. She knew that both girls had to be entirely willing at the outset, otherwise it could create problems later.

She left the two girls on the sidewalk and continued to prowl for new recruits for her mistress. Cynthia was only too well aware that she would get a severe beating from Santee Kimes if she did not deliver two slave girls.

Santee Kimes was a very strange woman. Her mood swings had become notorious in the Kimes' household. One minute she would be charming, then the next she would erupt into violence that was all too often directed at her servants — and that included Cynthia.

'I prefer them healthy, young and easy to manipulate,' Kimes had often told Cynthia, who suspected that some of the girls were sexual fantasy figures to Kimes, even though she had never actually witnessed any sexual attacks upon the women in the household.

Cynthia had watched Kimes lick her lips whenever new slave girls were recruited as 'domestic servants' in one of the Kimes' numerous households spread across America. She suspected that, at the very least, the girls provided some kind of fantasy kick for Kimes and her husband, Kenneth.

Back on the seedy streets of Tijuana that warm evening, Cynthia continued her hunt for new slaves for her mistress. Less than an hour later, she spotted another pair of girls — slightly older than the previous ones — and started her patter once again.

It emerged that the two girls were just out of school, unemployed but desperate for work and particularly keen on the idea of a fresh start across the border in cash-rich California. They were perfect.

Cynthia drove them to their parents' homes and explained the deal. She told them that the girls would be working for a very nice lady, as maids in her homes. It seemed like a dream come true to the families who were struggling to exist.

'We'll organise your papers once we get to La Jolla,' explained Cynthia to the bewildered girls before she opened the trunk of the Ford. 'But it's best if you hide in here until we get across the border.'

The girls looked at each other and giggled. It was an adventure and they had each other for protection.

What harm could possibly come to them?

Two hours later, Cynthia rolled up outside the Kimes' whitewashed, villa-style residence, just a stone's throw from the Pacific Ocean with her two new recruits ...

Santee Kimes smiled in anticipation when she saw the two young girls walking up to the house.

'Well, well,' she purred. 'They look perfect.'

Kimes told Cynthia to take the two girls to their room — a tiny box with just one single mattress for them both to sleep on.

When one of the girls complained, Cynthia told them that they would be given their own rooms within a few days, but for the moment they would have to make do.

'Is it possible to eat something?' asked one of the girls.

'Tomorrow. You must sleep first'

At 5.30am the next morning, the two girls were shaken by Cynthia.

'It's time to work. Come on.'

Neither of them stirred at first. Then Santee Kimes appeared, hands on hips and looking every inch the matriarch.

'Get up. NOW!'

The girls tried to pull down their skimpy T-shirts as they scrambled to their feet. Kimes stood over them hungrily.

'Move your butts. Get to it,' screeched their mistress. On the face of it, Santee Kimes was a most unlikely abuser of slaves. This attractive 41-year-old dark-haired wife of hotel chain owner Kenneth Kimes seemed to have everything she needed at her fingertips.

Her millionaire husband provided her with homes in La Jolla, Las Vegas, Hawaii, Washington DC and Cancun, Mexico. She had expensive cars, designer-label clothes and he allowed her to employ at least six servants at any one time.

But beneath Santee Kimes' veneer of respectability lay an increasing paranoia. She hated her husband's relatives whom she called 'creeps' and was becoming increasingly obsessed about them wanting to abduct her ten-year-old son.

'They travelled a great deal, moving from place to place to assure themselves privacy,' explained Santee Kimes' devoted friend, retired Californian law enforcement officer Grant Christopherson.

'Sometimes they registered under different names to make sure their enemies — the "creeps" — were not aware of where Santee was.'

Those fears of abduction, Kimes later claimed, were why she was so secretive and strict with her domestic servants.

Kimes even told her friend, Grant Christopherson, that someone had tried to grab her son while they were walking on a beach in Hawaii, but that Kimes had fought the assailant off and he had run away.

'There was also one episode when someone broke into her household in Hawaii and used what looked like blood to paint threatening signs on the wall,' added Christopherson.

The law enforcement officer even recalled how Kimes told him that she 'went into her car, closed the door and discovered rattle snakes in the car. She couldn't get the door open and had to break the window to get out'.

The cause of all this fear and tension seems to have been Kimes' husband Kenneth's business practices.

'Her husband was a very wealthy man and apparently money was the name of the game,' explained Christopherson's wife, Patricia. In short, Kenneth Kimes appeared to be mixing with some pretty tough gangsters. Kimes' numerous servants, hired throughout the early and mid-1980s, were in no doubt that they were being held at the Kimes' residences as slaves.

At the Kimes' home in Hawaii another girl, Adela Sanchez Guzman, found herself trapped in slavery. She was locked in her tiny bedroom at night and told that she was forbidden to leave the property for any reason. And when another maid was hired shortly after they arrived in Hawaii, Adela was forbidden even to speak to the girl. When Santee Kimes spotted the two women talking a few days later, she went berserk and beat Adela with a wooden coat-hanger.

'I told you not to speak to her. I told you,' Kimes kept repeating over and over again as she beat her slave girl.

Then she grabbed a wire coat-hanger and made Adela remove her jeans 'just to make sure you never forget my orders ever again'.

When Adela began crying, Kimes shouted at her, 'You can't leave here. You are going to be here for ever.' That was just the first of numerous beatings at the hands of her mistress. Kimes slapped Adela around the head and face virtually every day.

She would become particularly infuriated whenever she found Adela crying in her room.

As the weeks turned into months, Kimes got into

the habit of beating her slave girls whenever it took her fancy. Kimes would begin hyperventilating as soon as she started punishing her girls, suggesting that she was getting some pleasure out of the attacks.

Then one day, Kimes found a piece of paper on which the address of the house was written. She was furious.

'Come here, girl,' she screamed in Adela's direction. The terrified slave girl hesitantly moved towards her mistress. 'What is this?'

'Nothing,' came the reply.

'Nothing? It is our address. I think you were planning to give it to someone so that you could leave.'

'No, senora.'

'Yes, senora. You were planning to escape. I told you. You will never get away from here, so do not try.'

Santee Kimes' nostrils flared open. She snatched a man's belt from the drawer of a nearby desk.

'Lay your hand on the desk.'

'What?'

Kimes grabbed Adela's tiny wrists and smashed her hands down on the desk.

'Don't move.'

The first lash on her hand was the most painful. After that, everything seemed a blur.

In November, 1984, Kimes and her three current slave/maids travelled from her luxurious home in Hawaii to another family residence in Las Vegas.

One day, 21-year-old slave girl Maribel Cruz Ramirez was ironing her mistress's clothes when Kimes discovered a slip of paper with the telephone number of a maid she had met in Hawaii on it.

'Why the fuck have you got that, girl?' Kimes barked.

'It is my friend's number, senora.'

'I told you not to talk to anyone. Why have you defied me?'

Maribel was stunned. She knew what was coming next and she did not know how to handle it.

'Take off your clothes. NOW!'

Maribel hesitated. Then Kimes picked up the red hot iron and held it close to the slave girl's face. She was too frightened to speak.

Kimes then held the iron just above the girl's thigh and started to move it up ever so slowly

'Do it!'

Maribel began unbuttoning her blouse, distinctly aware of her mistress's heavy breathing. She watched as Kimes put the iron down and plugged it back in the socket.

'Faster, girl. Faster!'

When it came to her panties, Maribel hesitated.

'Everything.'

Standing there completely naked, the frightened servant feared the worse.

Just then, Kimes unplugged the iron.

Maribel covered her face with her hands and began to weep.

'Shut up!' screamed Kimes.

She held up the iron and pressed it against the back of Maribel's hands.

'Don't ever talk to anyone again. D'you understand, girl?'

'Yes, senora. Yes,' whimpered the slave girl.

Then she put the iron down and dragged Maribel along the corridor to the master bedroom. She was too scared to manage any resistance by this stage.

Kimes threw the naked girl on to the bed.

'Don't move.'

Kimes ripped open the door of her walk-in closet and pushed some of her clothes to one side.

She walked back to the young girl, grabbed her by the wrists once more and forced her into the closet.

'This is your bed for tonight. If you try to leave, I will kill you.'

Maribel watched in fear as the closet door slid shut. She could hear her mistress walking around the room. 'Just remember what I said. I don't want to hear a word from you.'

Maribel collapsed on the floor of the closet. She was too afraid to take any of her mistress's clothes to use as a bed, so she lay on the splintered wooden floor, naked, cold and miserable.

A couple of hours later, she heard Kimes giggling as she entered the bedroom with her husband. Maribel had no choice but to listen to their heated lovemaking. Her sick and twisted mistress was making particularly loud noises because she knew that one of her maids was locked, naked, in the closet.

During this period, it became clear to all those working in the Kimes household that Santee Kimes was becoming increasingly paranoid and horrifically sadistic. She insisted that she did not want anyone in her house to answer the door because she feared she was going to be served with a subpoena, but she never actually said what it related to.

'If people came to the door,' explained Melody Keltz, who was hired as a tutor for Kimes' son, 'Mrs Kimes said I should not answer. If someone approached me outside, I was to say I was a decorator. She said someone was trying to serve her and her husband with some kind of legal summons.'

Keltz continued, 'I was not to let the maids open the door, not to let them mail letters and not to let them leave the property. Mrs Kimes said I should treat the maids like little children. She said they were stupid.'

Once a maid got chickenpox and another tutor, Brownie Otto, took her to a doctor. When Kimes found out, she went berserk and beat both of them.

On another occasion, Kimes decided to show Otto 'how to treat the maids'. She went into the back yard of the huge house in Las Vegas where one maid was working and grabbed her by the hair and started shaking her.

Otto looked on in astonishment as Kimes gave her own running commentary.

'See? They don't respond. They are just so dumb.'

Then Otto was stunned when Kimes pulled the struggling maid over her knees and ripped open her jeans before pulling them down to her knees. She then proceeded to spank her bare bottom at least half a dozen times.

Melody Keltz left Kimes soon after a similar incident because 'I was not valued as a human being by her'. She later claimed she did nothing to report Kimes' brutal regime to the authorities because she feared that Kimes would kill her.

One beating was sparked off when a young slave girl burnt some toast. A few days later, Kimes pulled a loaded pistol on the maid and tried to force it into her mouth before being interrupted by the doorbell.

A third incident occurred in a hotel suite when the slave girl was accompanying her mistress on a trip.

Dolores explained, 'I had an allergy and my blood pressure rose and I fainted. La senora said to go into the bathroom.'

Kimes then forcibly stripped the girl of her clothes and pushed her into the steaming hot shower.

'I set the water at lukewarm but she changed it to very hot. It burned. When I moved away to a corner of the bathtub, she threw hot water on me from a little pot.' Once, yet another of Kimes' son's tutors was stunned to discover she was expected to help her employer smuggle more slave girls across the border.

Teresa Richards asked a cab driver in Tijuana to take her to a quiet crossing point where she saw a gap in the border fence and walked two prospective maids across the border.

Richards later explained, 'Mrs Kimes told me to treat the maids as if they were chairs. They were to be allowed no freedom.'

The tutor claimed she was virtually brainwashed, and feared that Kimes would go after her if she dared to leave her employment.

One of the few slave girls to get away from Kimes was feisty young latin Maria Salgado. She was just fourteen years old when Kimes picked her up in Mexico and offered her a job as a maid.

Within days of arriving in California, Maria was

hit across the face by Kimes, who objected to the way that the young girl had answered her back on a point of discipline.

When Maria tried to find a telephone in the house to call her family, she discovered part of it in a bureau drawer, and another part in a closet. She was just about to put the instrument together and plug it in when Kimes came in and immediately punished her with a severe beating on her backside.

Two days later, Maria broke a window and fled the house in La Jolla. She then reported her captivity to police officers and was eventually reunited with her parents.

The FBI, acting on information provided by Maria, arrested Kenneth and Santee Kimes at their La Jolla home in the summer of 1985.

Santee Kimes faced a trial in February 1986. But just a few weeks before the case got under way, she escaped from the lock-up section of the Southern Nevada Memorial Hospital, where she was undergoing medical tests.

Kimes was eventually re-arrested after four days on the run when US marshalls and FBI agents tracked her down to the parking lot of the Elbow Room Bar, in Las Vegas. She had spent her nights on the run sleeping under trees and anywhere else she could find shelter.

In a precedent-setting case in Nevada, Kimes was found guilty of fourteen out of sixteen counts of holding young women as slaves after the jury took nine hours to consider its verdict.

'Santee Kimes is a greedy, cunning and cruel woman who thought she was above the law,' assistant US attorney Karla Dobinski told the court in her closing statement. 'She lied to the maids to get them to go with her. She coerced them into staying with her by overcoming their will.'

Calling it one of the most unusual cases he had ever judged, US District Judge Howard McKibben sentenced slave-keeper Kimes to the maximum five-year prison term.

He also placed her husband, Kenneth Kimes, aged 67, on probation — suspending a three-year term except for a sixty-day period in an alcohol treatment centre — and imposed a £46,000 fine.

Judge McKibben said reports both from a government-appointed psychiatrist and another psychiatrist indicated that Santee Kirnes was in need of therapy. Noting that Kimes suffered from fairly substantial emotional disturbances,' he said that this had to be balanced against the 'reprehensible acts' for which she was convicted.

In June, 1986, four women employed by the convicted slave keeper and her husband filed suit against the couple for breach of contract, misrepresentation, emotional distress, assault and battery.

In July, 1991, the enslavement conviction against Santee Kimes was upheld by a federal appeals court.

She has now been freed and is believed to be living in California.

8

The El Monte Sweatshop

*'He who is by nature not his own but another's
man, is by nature a slave.'*

Aristotle

2614 Santa Anita Avenue, El Monte, Southern
California, August, 1995.

In the dense pre-dawn mist, no one noticed the
slight figure scrambling over the razor-wired wall of the
back yard of the nondescript apartment block on a busy
suburban street. The only noise was the occasional
distant purr of a V8 truck carrying some early shift
workers on their way to work.

WELCOME TO FRENDLY EL MONTE, read the
baby-blue-on-yellow sign planted at the kerb in front of
the apartment complex. Inside, scores of slave girls were

living a life of fear and degradation, beaten if they tried to complain about conditions.

Mariwan's heart was beating at a furious rate. The seconds were ticking away since the pretty young Thai woman had woken and slipped silently out of the first-floor window of the squalid dormitory that had been her home since arriving in California from Thailand almost three years earlier.

Just a few hours earlier, Mariwan had set out her escape plan in very cold and calculating terms. She had just been beaten by 'Pa', the foreman at the horrendous sweatshop where she had been enslaved since the day her feet touched American soil. This time she had truly had enough. She had to do something to close this hell-hole before somebody died.

All thoughts of the so-called 'American Dream' had long since disappeared. Mariwan, aged 26, and the seventy-one other women slaves at the sweatshop just wanted to go home to their families.

Their mistresses and masters were known by a variety of sick nicknames that would haunt the slave girls for the rest of their lives. There was 'Auntie', the evil elderly Thai woman who took great pleasure in beating many of them with a stick; then there was the awful 'Torn', supported by the pock-marked 'Porn' and a host of others. The men would often take it in turn to abuse their slaves.

On other occasions, the slave girls were proudly shown photographs of beaten women who had dared to try to escape from the El Monte labour camp. Many of the girls were told that if they disobeyed the regime inside the sweatshop they would be raped by Americans or Mexicans.

Some women were warned that their families would have their homes in Thailand destroyed if they did not obey their orders to work in these labour camps. Slave girls had even been forced to carry out do-it-yourself dental work on their own teeth.

Runaway Mariwan had concluded that anything was better than this living nightmare and even though she risked incarceration for having no legal travel documents, escape was her only hope. Naturally, Mariwan was worried that the bosses of the factory might come after her, but she knew there would be no turning back after she had made her getaway.

Once in the alley behind the apartment block, she continued running quietly along the edge of the wall, determined not to fail at the last hurdle. Mariwan thought she heard voices behind her, but it might have been from another building — it was impossible to tell. She just kept running.

The story that she had to tell the authorities sounded almost too incredible for words, considering the location was a quiet town in the most civilised nation on earth.

However, in the end, she was believed and a raid was mounted on the premises to liberate the slave girls and bring their masters and mistresses to justice.

The route that led to the sweatshop in El Monte, near Los Angeles, was, tragically, an all too familiar set-up: young Thai women were persuaded to pay unscrupulous agents in their homeland for travel and immigration documents with the promise of safe, secure, well-paid jobs on their arrival in the USA.

Instead, they were herded onto buses at LA's International Airport, taken directly to the El Monte sweatshop and coerced into working.

Once the workers arrived at the so-called 'factory', the sweatshop bosses seized their passports and took back the 'show money' that had been provided for them as a cover, should US Immigration officials question them about their planned tourist itineraries.

'It soon became crystal clear that they were working in a virtual labour camp,' said one investigator who took part in the initial raid on the building.

Not only were the workers prevented from leaving the premises, but their slave masters and mistresses barred them from communicating with one another. The workers actually believed they were working off travel debts of $5,000 (£3,000).

They were held in the guarded complex and forced to work from 7am to midnight, seven days a week for less than $2 (£1.30) an hour — and that money was simply deducted from their supposed debts to their slave masters.

According to many of the slave girls, it was always baking hot inside the factory where they were mainly expected to sew seams and collars, Hawaiian shirts and surfer shorts. In the words of the most serious of the charges that their mistresses and masters would eventually face, 'they were unlawfully inveigled, decoyed, seized, confined, kidnapped and abducted' to their hellish jobs.

Yet El Monte itself could not be further removed from the sort of place where one would expect slavery to thrive with such intensity and, apparently, with little interference from the local population.

This working-class community of 110,000 prided itself on functioning more like a family than a city. When wagon-train pioneers from the Midwest came looking for gold in the 1850s, El Monte was their oasis. The early settlement, bordered by Rio Hondo and the San Gabriel River, was lush with a plentiful water supply and vegetation. It became known as 'El Monte, the end of the Santa Fe Trail'.

Yet, for those seventy-two slave girls who toiled in a factory disguised as an apartment block, it was hell.

The town where most children attended El Monte High School, married their childhood sweethearts, and settled down to lead a long, simple life, chose to turn its back on the poor, innocent women entrapped by nine evil slave masters.

But then, 1995 was not a good year for El Monte. The discovery of the sweatshop was only the latest high-profile news to tarnish the city's reputation. In February, the Dahlia Gardens Guest Home for the mentally ill came under fire after one resident beat another to death with a rock. Then in April, five people, including an infant and a five-year-old girl, were shot dead, execution style, in their El Monte home.

Even after the discovery of the sweatshop — one of the biggest enforced-labour camps ever uncovered in peace time — local dignitaries insisted that it could have been set up anywhere.

Yet others in the community were outraged that the sweatshop went unnoticed for so long.

'How the hell could no one have noticed it? The

place was surrounded by razor wire. I don't think anyone wanted to know about a bunch of Thais,' reckons one local resident.

Local Police Chief Wayne Clayton defended his 131-member force, saying his officers lacked the authority to go door-to-door inspecting every business. 'That sweatshop was housed very close to the corner on Santa Anita Avenue, one of our busiest streets. Nobody recognised it. When you drive by, you can almost touch it.'

Two weeks after the raid on the El Monte sweatshop, a federal grand jury indicted nine alleged operators of the slave business, charging that the forced-labour ring recruited workers in Thailand, smuggled them into the United States, confined them under threat, censored their mail and monitored their telephone calls.

All nine defendants were charged with conspiracy and concealing and harbouring illegal immigrants. The accused could face up to five years in prison and $250,000 (£170,000) fines on each of the charges.

Among those charged was a Thai fugitive called Sukit Manasurangkul, aged 40, who, the indictment stated, helped recruit the workers in Thailand. An arrest warrant was issued for Manasurangkul, known to some workers as 'Sunshine', who is still believed to be on the run in Thailand.

Seven of the suspects are said to be related, including four who may be the sons of the woman believed to be the ringleader — Suni Manasurangkul, 65, whom workers referred to as 'Auntie'. She allegedly ran the El Monte operation in matriarchal style, giving her slave girls working and sleeping assignments and warning them that they were not free to leave. She would often resort to violence if any of the women defied her.

Others in custody included two alleged guards at the El Monte complex and two women believed to be daughters-in-law of Manasurangkul.

Within a month of the raid, US and Californian officials filed lawsuits claiming some $5 million in back wages due to the former workers, who were freed from immigration custody within a week of the swoop. They were to serve as key witnesses in the criminal case against the sweatshop operators.

Others charged were Tavee Uvawas, 35; Sunton Rawungchaisong, 30; Rampa Suthaparasit, 32; Suporn Verayutwilai, 29; Seree Granjapiree, 28; Hong Wangdee, and Thanes Panthong, 30.

Incredibly, it was then disclosed that many of Los Angeles' most successful garment manufacturers had used the sweatshop to make goods.

Some retailers reacted strongly on hearing that they might be stocking garments made in the sweatshop. 'We will not tolerate conditions identified during the El Monte raid,' declared Bernard F Brennan, chairman and chief executive officer of Montgomery Ward, the largest privately held retainer in the USA which immediately removed all 'New Boys' merchandising from sales floors nationwide. Other stores soon followed suit.

In contrast to the deplorable conditions of the El Monte sweatshop, the workers were housed in a fully equipped detention centre following the raid on the 'factory'.

Immigration and Naturalization Service spokesman Ron Rogers said, 'They're getting three hot meals a day and a bed, and medical treatment is available.'

The most tragic aspect of the El Monte sweatshop is that there are millions more women where those ones came from. They are all too often poor, naive, single and defenceless. There is always a 'Mr Big' lording it over them, a pimp, whether or not they work in the sex trade. It might be a cruel employer, a corrupt cop, a mindless bureaucrat — or even a parent.

Even when one of them managed to slip out of that razor-wired hell-hole initially no one really wanted to hear her story.

Now these women's accounts are going to be heard. They will get their day in court and many of them have already got new, legal jobs in California.

'They want to be as independent and self-sufficient as possible,' explained Chanchanit Martorell, executive director of the Thai Community Development Center, one of a handful of civilian groups who helped look after the slave girls following their liberation.

'It's been really hard for them to stay idle because they're so used to working.'

Some of the slave girls even returned to garment factories. Others sought domestic work. The Thai community centre helped to place the workers in new jobs, and screened each potential post to ensure it offered at least the minimum wage and a safe environment.

The women also savoured their first taste of freedom in the USA with visits to Disneyland and a specially held beachfront barbecue in Malibu.

Federal agents swooped on three more suspected sweatshops in the Los Angeles area and arrested fifty-five people including thirty-nine Thai workers. It even emerged that Disney was among the companies that marketed clothing manufactured in those alleged sweatshops, uncovered shortly after the El Monte raid. Interviews with workers at the sites produced definite evidence of violations of minimum wage, overtime, child labour and record-keeping regulations, according to Labor Investigators.

The US Immigration Service believes that the Thai nationals at these three new sites were also smuggled in and employed in a form of debt.

All three sweatshops were in largely immigrant areas of downtown Los Angeles, and officials claimed that many of the workers appeared to have been 'coached in what to say' by their supervisors.

The El Monte raid and these subsequent swoops appear to have highlighted a huge problem in southern California, where there are estimated to be more than 100,000 underpaid workers employed in the highly competitive garment industry.

Meanwhile, the reverberations from the El Monte raid continue to rumble.

California Governor Pete Wilson became involved when he demanded that US Attorney General Janet Reno investigate the alleged indifference of the US Immigration and Naturalisation Service and the US Attorney's office in Los Angeles for their failure to close down the El Monte sweatshop sooner.

But as one legitimate Thai businessman in LA commented, 'We all know this is just the tip of the iceberg. The sweatshops are everywhere and a few raids isn't going to get rid of them overnight.'

9

Casualty of War

*'This is what it means / to be a slave: to be abused
and bear it / compelled by violence to suffer wrong.'*

Euripides, 425 BC

Arok, Sudan, Summer, 1990.

Meiram was just fourteen years old when she
found herself orphaned after Sudanese nomads, armed
with machine guns and rocket-propelled grenades,
attacked her home village in the south of this desolate
country.

As the young girl fled north with her sister and
grandmother, they were captured by another group of
armed nomads, or 'Murahaleen' as they are known
locally. Meiram managed to escape their clutches after
one of the soldiers raped her and then fell asleep. She

could hear other militia doing the same to her sister and grandma, but she knew she had to run for her life. The guilt of leaving behind her only two relatives would stay with her for ever.

After three days of wandering through the desert, Meiram came across another band of nomads. At first she presumed they would abuse her as the other nomads had, but this group seemed more civilised than those she had previously encountered.

They let her share their water and food and expected nothing in return. She rode their camels as they progressed through the desert and, for the first time in many months, she started to believe that life was worth living.

One of the leaders of the nomads called himself Bona and he seemed particularly concerned with Meiram's welfare. Whenever any of the other nomads took anything more than a passing interest in the young girl, he would gallantly ward them off.

Meiram felt she had found a family to replace her own, whom she presumed to have been brutally killed during that earlier attack.

Bona gave Meiram back her self-respect. She began to gain some confidence and he even started to help her to read and write as the band of nomads travelled through the southern region of the country.

At night, Meiram was allowed to sleep alone and Bona issued a warning to all the other nomads not to try to sleep with her or they would have to face his fury. Many of the younger nomads believed that Meiram was being 'kept fresh' for Bona to have later when he reached their final destination.

But when the Murahaleen reached a busy desert outpost, Bona started barking orders at Meiram to make herself look perfectly groomed.

'You must look clean and healthy in such a place as this, otherwise the other women will look down on you,' he assured her in a fatherly fashion.

However, Bona was actually preparing Meiram to be sold as a slave girl to the highest bidder.

She did not realise what was happening until it was too late. Bona never spoke to her again. She saw his self-satisfied face as she was taken away by two male servants who worked for her new 'owner' — a steely-eyed Arab called Mahmoud, who had paid Bona 4,000 Sudanese pounds (about £200) for her.

To make matters even worse, the town where she had been stranded was right in the middle of the combat zone of Sudan's seven-year-old civil war.

'I felt betrayed, alone and terrified. In the past few months I had lost my family, my self-respect, my dignity and now my freedom,' recalled Meiram.

To start with, the young slave girl was expected to wash and clean for her new master, living under the constant fear of being killed if she did not work efficiently enough for him.

She received no money and precious little food, other than occasional scraps from the remains of the servants' meals.

When there was a distribution of relief food for the nation's millions of starving people nearby, Meiram's master forbade her to attend.

The only thing she had held on to was her body; he made no attempt to molest her and she was at least thankful for that.

But in an effort to get some real food, Meiram was forced to go and beg in the nearby market, which only opened when the bombing raids ceased. She would humbly hold out a begging bowl for hours on end and be extremely lucky if she raised enough money to buy a piece of fruit.

Back at her master's home, she was becoming increasingly withdrawn and unresponsive to Mahinoud's orders. He started to beat her regularly with a stick. But this punishment did have one positive repurcussion: Mahmoud would feel so guilty afterwards that he would let Meiram have the pick of the fruit bowl, once he had gorged himself.

Although Meiram did not realise it, slavery had become a common occurrence in the Sudan in the late 1980s. Firsthand accounts from the southern Dinka people suggested that the classic ingredients of slavery — captivity, unpaid labour, beatings and sale — were widespread. Young female slaves — many not yet in their teens — were bought and sold like cattle for purely sexual purposes, as Meiram was about to find out. For when the Arab decided to move on to the town of Arok, he took her with him and decided to buy himself another young girl.

'You look too tatty and thin to be the sort of slave girl I really want,' he told Meiram. It seemed that his meanness towards her had actually saved her from having to make the ultimate sacrifice.

But when they got to Arok, Mahinoud could not find a suitable girl. Understandably, Meiram became concerned. She felt torn because she did not want to be his sex slave, but she also feared for any other girl who fell into his clutches. However, in the end she had no choice.

On the second night of their stay in Arok, her Arab master slept in his own tent while she slept with just a sheet for cover outside. Ever since their arrival in the town, she had barely slept a wink for fear that he might try to rape her during the night. 'I was so confused and scared. I did not want to submit to his demands but I needed him to survive. I just prayed that he would not come after me,' she later explained.

At about 4am, Meiram finally fell into a troubled sleep. Her only weapon of defence was a stone she had picked up from the roadside the previous day.

'Don't move. Just lie still,' a harsh voice whispered in her ear.

Meiram tried to move but he had her pinned down. She struggled for breath. His hand covered her mouth.

'Quiet!'

As her eyes adjusted to the dark, she could just make out the face. It was not her master. But then a voice came out of the dark.

'Hurry up. Get a move on.'

That was definitely her master. She tried to move her head in the direction of his voice. She just caught a glance of him out of the corner of her eye before the man above her forced her head round straight again.

'Don't move, slave girl.'

Just then, frightened Meiram became aware of at least three pairs of eyes watching her in the darkness. She had just become the sex toy of three evil men, including her master.

For the next three months, Meiram was passed from man to man, often expected to sleep with all three in one evening. They fed her continually in an effort to fatten her up. At first she could not resist the food, but as soon as she realised that the fatter she got the better they liked her, she started secretly to spit it out once they were out of sight. It was especially hard to spit out the tasty meat and vegetables because she was so hungry most of the time.

Meiram later discovered that Mahmoud had intended to use her as his sex slave with the two other men all along, but he had agreed not to sleep with her until they joined him and paid their share of her purchase price.

One of the other men treated her particularly roughly and would try to perform appalling acts of degradation on her virtually every night.

Sometimes Mahmoud would almost show sympathy for her by warning the man not to hurt her, but Meiram realised that he was only trying to protect his 'investment'. She knew the day would eventually come when they would try to sell her on to other men.

She even heard them saying one day that, with any luck, they could recoup at least what they had paid for her because she was still so young.

In every town they passed through, Meiram lived in fear of being sold on to an even more brutal group of men. At least these three fed her and — after Mahmoud's intervention — the nastiest of the men had stopped forcing her to have painful, unlubricated anal sex.

The situation was not helped by the fact that the Sudanese Government continued to arm virtually all of its northern nomadic tribesmen, notably the Rizeigat and the Misseriya, creating Wild West-type shoot-outs on a regular, terrifying basis. Reports by the human rights organisations Africa Watch and Amnesty International provided evidence that such tribesmen had been armed to the teeth and given intelligence information about rival nomads by various government departments seeking to win Sudan's civil war on the cheap. By encouraging attacks on peoples such as the Dinkas, the government in Khartoum sought to debilitate a group that provided crucial support for the rebel Sudanese People's Liberation Army.

But none of this mattered to poor, innocent, young Meiram. Her only priority was to survive in the desert. She had even taken to wrapping herself in double the amount of clothing to try to hide her shapely figure in the hope it might put off her three 'husbands'. However, they were not that easily dissuaded. Their nightly demands continued unabated.

During stopovers in towns, Meiram heard stories from other slaves about even worse situations than the one she found herself in. One man — a Dinka — told her how he had been captured and sold twice, first for 100 Sudanese pounds (about £5), then for 220 Sudanese pounds (about £11). He claimed that his second buyer castrated him and branded him with an iron used to brand cows. The man told Meiram that many other Dinka men had been castrated.

In the Sudan, slave prices followed very basic rules of supply and demand. The greatest demand — as in the nineteenth century when the demand for slaves and ivory wrought widespread destruction on southern Sudan — appeared to be for adolescents and young women.

On her travels, Meiram even encountered liberated slaves who warned her that the only way she could gain her freedom would be if a relative reclaimed her — and then that would require a bribe to the local police.

Poor Meiram did not have a single living relative. Her situation seemed hopeless. Even the tears she had shed every night after letting her three masters have sex with her had dried up. Her emotions were numbed by despair.

She felt thoroughly used, abused and discarded. She no longer trusted anyone. The three men who took it in turns to sleep with her had become — in a twisted way — her only protectors.

For the first few months of her 'marriage' to the threesome, they had often handcuffed her at night to stop her trying to escape and to make it easier to force themselves on her. But, after a while, they mistook her resignation as a sign of compliance and they stopped manacling her at night. To begin with, this newly gained freedom did not provoke any response from the defeated young slave girl.

The evenings had taken on a pattern. As night fell, Meiram would be given a bowl of food to build up her strength for the coming sexual activities; sometimes even a glass of illicit home-brewed alcohol to win her over. Then Mahmoud would always be the first to start fumbling with her. And so it went on.

However, on one particular evening when the

third of her masters had crawled on her as she lay there, resigned to her fate, she got a nasty surprise — he had brought a friend along and insisted that she should also have sex with him.

Meiram was outraged by the suggestion. Her protestations were naturally ignored, but the indignity of having a complete stranger introduced to the proceedings suddenly awoke the spirit within her.

'How dare they treat me like this!' she stormed. How could she have just lain there for all those months and done nothing?

Meiram was more angry with herself than anyone else. She started to tense when the stranger mounted her, then she relaxed. She decided there and then to make her escape that night and she did not intend to give them an excuse to put her back in shackles again.

That night, Meiram waited until she was sure all four men were fast asleep in their tents. She even counted the snores and the snorts to be absolutely sure, as she knew this might be her only chance.

The men were complacent about their captive because they knew she had nowhere to run and therefore would never dare escape from their clutches. But they had not counted on her determination.

Meiram silently gathered up her few belongings and headed for the outskirts of the small town where they were staying at the time. 'I had no idea where we were but I knew I just had to keep heading north, where it was safer,' she later recalled.

Meiram took immediate advantage of the dark, moonless night and let the stars guide her as far north of the town as she could get before dawn.

Then, as the sun rose, she climbed the nearest bushy tree to hide until sunset.

'It was the only way I stood a chance,' she explained.

The first two days on the run were definitely the most risky because Meiram feared that every person she passed might be heading for that same town and maybe tell her masters they had seen her going north.

On the second day, Meiram was hiding in a tall tree when she heard two men talking below and she became convinced they were looking for her. She never knew for sure whether that was just her own understandable paranoia but she became even more cautious on her journey the following night.

After six hard days of travelling, she reached a relatively friendly outpost which had remained virtually unaffected by the war. The first person she met was a woman who was looking for a housekeeper to look after her baby. Meiram — who had once had baby sisters of her own — leapt at the chance and thanked her lucky stars for being alive. Maybe life was worth living after all.

Enslavement in the Sudan region is rooted in religion. Many of the Dinka people are Christians; only a few are Muslim. Government radio broadcasts at the time of the Civil War actually endorsed the military raids as a 'jihad against the pagans'. Among the Misseriya, the word 'abide', meaning slave, has been used to refer not only to domestic slaves but also to those who, because they were non-Muslims, could have been appropriately captured and turned into slaves.

As one human rights activist in the Sudan

commented, 'If the governments of the USA and Britain have normal relations with the government of Sudan, they are condoning slavery.'

With Western governments still attaching low priority to human rights issues in the Sudan, many observers fear that the residents of the south of the country will continue to pay a heavy price ...

10

Wages of Fear

'Machines are worshipped because they are beautiful, and valued because they confer power; they are hated because they are hideous, and loathed because they impose slavery.'

Bertrand Russell, 1928

Marina Drive, Quincy, Near Boston, 28 August, 1992.

'You will not walk alone outside the apartment.'

'Why not?' Vasantha Gedara asked her new employer.

'Because the police will kill you or a stranger will rape you.'

'Oh ...'

Perhaps Vasantha should have taken heed of that warning and realised that it was a good indication of the problems that were to follow, but she was a 22-year-old woman in desperate need of a job and Kuwaiti Talal

Aizanki seemed like a responsible person. She had even worked for his mother back in the Middle East.

He was a 30-year-old Boston University electrical engineering graduate with a pregnant 21-year-old wife whom he seemed genuinely to love and adore.

Sri Lankan maid Vasantha was fully aware that Kuwaitis were not always the easiest people in the world to work for, but she was now in the United States of America so it could not possibly end up like one of those horror stories she had come across in the Middle East. Little did she realise that the journey she had just made from Boston's Logan International Airport was the last time she would be allowed outdoors for four months.

When Alzanki showed Vasantha to her room, she was in for yet another surprise. There was no bed, not even a mattress, and her 'room' was actually a corner of the hallway.

Alzanki explained calmly, yet coldly, 'You are not permitted to sit on the furniture.'

'But I cannot sleep without a mattress.'

'Too bad.'

Something about his attitude told Vasantha not to argue with Aizanki that day. She needed the job badly and, hopefully, her new employers would mellow as time passed. She did not even object when he insisted that she hand over her money and passport 'for safe keeping' the moment she entered the apartment.

The first few days in the Alzanki apartment in the Boston suburb of Quincy were very quiet. Neither husband nor wife seemed to say much to each other and Mrs Alzanki was forbidden from talking to her maid.

Vasantha tried to get on with the jobs Mr Alzanki had described when she first went for the interview for the job.

Aizanki tended to work long hours at the university and his strictly Muslim wife was not permitted to leave the apartment unless accompanied by her husband.

One of the first big mistakes that Vasantha made was to be caught sitting down on a kitchen chair when the master of the house came back from the university Without any pleasantries, Alzanki steamed right in.

'Get off that chair. I told you not to use any of the furniture. If you disobey me again, you will die!'

Vasantha was petrified by this threat but decided that since he had asked her not to use the furniture when she started, she would concede to him this time. She scuttled off to her bare, tiny living area and tried to bury herself in a book.

Suddenly, she heard Alzanki shouting and screaming at the top of his voice. He was speaking Arabic to his wife but she could tell it was not a polite conversation. This was an angry exchange of words.

Just as quickly, there was complete silence. Vasantha thought nothing more about it until she suddenly heard an almighty crash and a loud scream from Mrs Alzanki. She rushed out of her corner of the hall and was going through the kitchen towards the sitting-room when AIzanki came charging towards her.

'Get back in your room. Now!'

Vasantha turned around, convinced that he was about to hit her next, unless she did as she was told.

The following 111 days at that Quincy apartment

turned into a nightmare of human degradation and enslavement that was worse than anything seen in Boston for at least a hundred years.

After about two weeks, Vasantha 'dared' to enquire about when her promised wages would start being paid. 'You will be paid when I decide to pay you,' came the reply.

She was not allowed to make any phonecalls and was forbidden from looking out of the window or stepping outside. At Thanksgiving weekend in November, 1992, the Alzankis announced they were going upstate to visit some friends and Vasantha was 'not to leave the apartment under any circumstances'.

'There's pitta bread and some fresh water in the refrigerator,' barked AIzanki in his imperious tone. That was all Vasantha had ever been offered to eat. She looked aghast. He noticed her expression and added, 'If you leave the apartment I will know ... and remember what I told you about the police. They will shoot a single woman out at night in this neighbourhood.'

When the Alzankis returned from their Thanksgiving weekend, things went from bad to worse. The master of the house insisted that Vasantha use a particularly noxious cleaning chemical to scour the entire apartment from top to bottom. The liquid was almost pure acid and before long, her eyes were running profusely and she was in a lot of pain.

About two-thirds of the way through her cleaning duties, she fainted and cut her head on a table leg as she fell. The Alzankis refused her request to call a doctor when she recovered consciousness.

By the late autumn of 1992, the couple had banned Vasantha from mailing any letters to her family back home.

Mr Alzanki also reminded Vasantha that, because her job with them had been arranged through a Kuwaiti employment agency, they were perfectly within their rights to put her on a plane back to the Middle East if she did not perform her duties satisfactorily.

With this threat ringing in her ears and an overwhelming fear of returning to Kuwait, Vasantha felt obliged to struggle on with this nightmare couple.

Throughout most of Vasantha's time at the house, Mrs Alzanki had remained fairly quiet and reserved and Vasantha presumed that her reluctance to speak was due to a scant knowledge of English. She could not have been more wrong.

On 17 December, 1992, Mrs Alzanki became incredibly angry with her slave girl after she accidentally dropped a plate on the kitchen floor.

'Next time, I will sew your mouth shut and kill you,' she screamed at her servant Not surprisingly, Vasantha was terrified.

Vasantha's duties at the Alzanki apartment were taking on monumental proportions. She was now cleaning the bathroom at least four times a day and replacing shelf paper in the kitchen cupboards daily. She was also forced to clean the carpets with a broom and wash clothes and dishes by hand, even though machines were available.

She was even denied dental treatment for an abscessed tooth, which eventually fell out.

Her paltry wage of $4.50 (£3) a day had still not

materialised.

After the birth of the Alzankis' son, life inside the apartment became slightly easier, if only because of the two friendly nurses who worked shifts looking after the infant. Both of them were horrified at the way the Alzankis treated Vasantha. One of them commented, 'They're treating you like an animal. It's disgraceful.'

Eventually, the two nurses hatched a plan to get Vasantha safely out of the apartment and into the nearest police station to report the full story of her horrific experiences. 'You've either got to go to the police or your local consul. Someone has to be told what these people are doing to you.'

Over the next few weeks, the scheme was carefully thought through as the two nurses smuggled in proper food for Vasantha and contacted a friendly policeman to take on the case.

The Alzankis were arrested by FBI agents on slavery charges for allegedly forcing Vasantha to work against her will, while paying her little and depriving her of food. They were also charged with conspiracy and involuntary servitude in a federal indictment that detailed a long list of abuses against Vasantha Gedara during the four-month period she worked for them.

She was in the country legally while working for the Alzankis, but became an illegal immigrant after leaving their home. She then applied for political asylum and received a work authorisation permit. The Alzankis, it emerged, were in the USA on a student visa.

Shortly after their arrest, Theodore Merritt and Steven M Dettelbach, a civil rights attorney with the

Justice Department, urged a magistrate to hold Talal Alzanki without bail until trial.

In a chaotic scene, Mrs Alzanki started sobbing uncontrollably when US Magistrate-Judge Lawrence P Cohen ordered him detained until a detention hearing at noon the next day. Mrs Alzanki was to be confined to her apartment under so-called house arrest. Prosecutors were told that her culture prohibited her from being separated from her husband and that she must return to Kuwait if he was jailed.

'It is going to be very difficult for me to take care of myself without Talal,' she sobbed to the court. 'I can't live without Talal. How will I support myself? Since he hasn't been proved guilty, why do you want to incarcerate him today?' she implored.

To make matters worse, Mrs Alzanki did not drive and could not, under Kuwaiti custom, be driven home by a strange man.

Prosecutors called it 'a case of modern-day slavery enforced by fear'. Defence lawyers contended that Vasantha had always been free to leave and that she was just a lonely maid stuck in a bad job.

In May, 1994, Alzanki was found guilty of enslaving Vasantha and ordered to serve one year and a day in prison for involuntary servitude and to pay Vasantha $13,400 (£9,000) in back wages.

Alzanki had been in line for an 18-24-month prison term under federal sentencing guidelines, but US District Judge Rya Zobel said she had considered the hardship Alzanki's imprisonment would impose on his wife, who had given birth to another child by the time the case came to trial.

Earlier, Alzanki himself had insisted that he was fully satisfied with Vasantha's work and her cooking and that she had over-reacted to his rules. However, jurist Patricia Hurley said of Alzanki's testimony, 'We didn't believe a word he said.'

The case against Mrs Alzanki had ended in a mistrial the previous week after she gave birth to the new baby.

US attorney Donald K Stern said, 'The jury's verdict makes clear that the most vulnerable of people deserve no less than our vigorous efforts.' Vasantha's lawyer, Sarah Burgess Reed, said her client was elated by the verdict. She is now employed as a nanny by an American family in Massachusetts.

The American Nightmare

'Slavery is the status or condition of a person over whom any or all of the powers attaching to the right of ownership are exercised.'

Article 1(i) Of The League Of Nations Convention On Slavery, Servitude, Forced Labour And Similar Institutions And Practices, 1926

New York City, April, 1994.

Her hair was thick, lustrous and dark as the night. Her shoulders and back were slender. Her legs were perfect, except for the occasional bruise dotted along the inside of her thighs.

But then petite Na had got used to pain since her arrival in the United States just twelve months earlier from Bangkok. During that period she had been forced to have sex with hundreds of men in a brothel/prison run by a gang of Chinese immigrants.

For Na, the American Dream had turned into a

nightmare from which there seemed no escape. Every bone in her body ached. She had become numbed by the brutal sexual encounters and had rapidly concluded that there was no goodness in the world, even beyond the four cruel walls of that building in Manhattan where she had been incarcerated for so long.

Some days, she would suffer humiliating torture at the hands of savage, uncaring clients who saw her as a sex toy. On the good days, they would not beat her. It had got so bad that requests for straight sex were met by Na with an overwhelming sense of relief.

Na's nightmare began when she was halfheartedly helping out in her parents' grocery store in the Thai capital of Bangkok, day-dreaming about a serious office job and a better life beyond the slums of one of the poorest cities in the world.

A local businessman walked into the store one day and made her a seemingly irresistible offer: he would arrange her passage to the United States and a job. It would not cost anything because her future employer would pay her expenses.

A few days later, Na was greeted at JFK Airport by two neatly dressed Chinese businessman in dark suits and immediately informed of the real Faustian terms of her passage to the Big Apple. To pay off the people who had bought her ticket and arranged her visa, she was expected to work in a brothel and have sex with hundreds of men.

Na was terrified. Then the men pointed out that she had no choice. They had her return ticket and her passport. They assured her that after she had sex with

300 men, her 'debt' would effectively be repaid and she would be free to go.

Then they informed her of her new life: she would be held captive behind the locked doors of a Chinatown brothel where the 'inmates' were known by numbers instead of names, bars covered the windows and buzzer-operated gates controlled the doors. She would not be allowed to leave the building until she had worked off that 'debt'.

Na began weeping in the Lincoln limousine as it whisked her towards her horrific new life. The two Chinese businessmen sat stony-faced and told her, 'You have no choice.'

Later she recalled, 'I was stunned. I cried until they threatened to beat me if I did not shut up. I thought: "I can't do anything. I am here. I can't do anything. I'm in their hands." '

What Na did not realise was that she was just one of an estimated TWO THOUSAND women held captive in the Chinatown district of New York alone. When she was bundled out of the Lincoln and escorted into the dimly-lit brothel/prison that would be her home for the following twelve months, she was shocked to discover thirty other women working in that cramped building under the supervision of a madam called Siew Geok Adkins, better known to the girls and their clients as Lilly Chan or Jenny. A bouncer was on duty the whole day and night to ensure that none of the girls tried to escape.

'You will stay downstairs until a man picks you for sex, then you will take him to any of the spare rooms,' Lilly Chan told the terrified Na within minutes of her arrival from the airport.

Just hours later, the first of literally hundreds of men she would encounter came up the stairs from the sleazy street below. Na tried to hide her pretty face by holding her head down in shame, but Lilly Chin snapped at her, 'Hold your head up, girl, or else I will tell them you are not working properly.'

Dazed and jet lagged from her long journey, Na could barely focus on the grinning figure who stood inspecting her and the other girls sitting around the lounge area of the brothel. She desperately tried to avoid his gaze in the hope he would pick another girl. But she could feel his eyes burning in her direction.

'You,' said the man. 'You. I want you.'

Na did not move at first Then one of the girls sitting next to her nudged her, 'He wants you'.

Na looked and tried to force a smile, fearful that she would be punished later if she did not respond. She got up and felt a cold shiver run down her spine as the man grabbed her hand as if they were sweethearts rather than strangers.

Madam Lilly Chan led the couple up a rickety staircase towards a damp, dingy cubicle with a low-slung single bed over which a filthy towel was unceremoniously draped. She snapped the rates at the man and then shut the door behind them.

The noise of sex from the other cubicles drifted across like a sick version of piped music in a restaurant Na tried to look away as the man undressed. She thought about her life at her parents' grocery store back in Bangkok and wondered why on earth she had ever thought it was boring.

'Bend over,' said the man, dragging poor Na back to the awful reality of her situation.

Ten minutes later, she reappeared in the lounge area of the brothel with red eyes and a broken spirit Her American Dream had just begun...

Life on the Bowery in the centre of Chinatown went from bad to worse for poor Na and the other captive women at the brothel. The cubicles in which they were expected to have sex with clients were filthy and draughty. In each one, a cardboard box of the cheapest condoms lay open on the floor.

Nearby, bouncer Joseph Morales — fat and sweaty — stood guard to ensure that none of the women tried to escape and that their clients never got more than they paid for. Every night, Morales was allowed by Lilly Chan to pick one girl for a free bout of sex as part of his 'fee' for working in the brothel. Na was one of his favourites. Virtually all of the women working at the building had been lured by the same sort of promises as Na. The 'businessmen' who greeted her at the airport had, a year earlier, switched their attention to Thai girls after finding that their regular supply of Korean, Taiwanese and Hong Kong prostitutes had dried up.

Customers paid a $30 (£20) admission fee and $100 (£65) for about an hour, although thankfully for the girls many of them were in and out within ten minutes. The women were expected to work from 11am to 4am every day of the week and Na had sex with, on average, two men every night.

For the first few weeks of Na's nightmare, she faced an angry backlash from customers and Lilly Chan because she was so sexually inexperienced. At one stage, Lilly Chan actually sat the terrified young girl down and told her how to satisfy a man. It sickened the poor girl to her stomach. Sometimes, Na was expected to go with two men at the same time. She never received any payment. Instead, it went towards 'paying off' her airfare and accommodation.

Little did Na realise that some of the girls working in that brothel had been bought outright by evil Madam Lilly Chan from the businessmen who provided them. She later admitted paying between $6,000 (£4,000) and $15,000 (£10,000) for many of the girls. One woman whom she had bought for $9,000 (£6,000) had to pay her back in 270 quotas — 270 men for $27,000 (£18,000). Other women — like Na — had to repay their smugglers by having sex with between 380 and 500 men. All were charged $300 (£200) a week for room and board, payable through sex with three more men.

The prostitutes kept track of how many men they had slept with in little notebooks. Lilly Chan kept a master ledger so that there were no disputes later over figures.

As the months passed by, Na found herself unable to fight back against the oppressive regime that now ruled her unhappy life. Her sexual encounters with complete strangers were becoming increasingly dangerous as many of the men demanded sadistic practices.

Bruising was becoming commonplace. Sometimes the clients would bite her and then she would spend weeks fearful that she had caught AIDS or some other disease.

Her spirit was crushed. Her determination to fight

back had disappeared and she could see no light at the end of the tunnel.

Some of the other girls talked about escaping and going to the authorities, but most of them were convinced they would receive little or no sympathy. The girls considered themselves sordid hookers about whom the outside world would rather not know.

Madam Lilly Chan regularly told them that they were worthless and they would be lucky to be deported if detained by the immigration authorities. It was much more likely that they would be arrested and sent to prison. Most of the girls believed her.

And any doubts that some of the stronger girls harboured were soon destroyed when Lilly Chan told them gleefully about how a girl who had escaped from a nearby brothel had been murdered because she had threatened to go to the authorities.

It was not as if the police did not know what was going on at brothels such as the one on the Bowery. But coerced prostitution of foreign women is especially difficult to combat because of its secrecy and the profit that drives it. In any case, it was virtually impossible to prove because the prostitutes often feared revenge and deportation and so would not agree to testify against their slave masters.

Back at the brothel, Na and many of the other girls were suffering as badly as ever. Their only meal each day was a meagre bowl of rice and some chicken soup if they were lucky.

When she had been there about nine months, one of the other girls was badly beaten by a client. Lilly Chan would not allow the girl to be taken to hospital for treatment, so a Chinese doctor was brought in. 'But he was useless and we all ended up nursing her back to health,' explained Na. The attack on the girl made the other inmates of the brothel even more fearful for their own safety.

Eventually, city inspectors decided to try to close the building on the basis of housing code violations, since they had long given up any hope of proving it was a brothel. Checking the premises on 11 October, 1994, they encountered two women — amongst thirty-one in the brothel at that time — who made it clear they wanted to leave.

That was enough of an excuse for the police to get involved once again and it also attracted interest from the immigration service. But the authorities soon discovered that their efforts were fruitless because all the other women — including a terrified Na — were unwilling to speak out against Lilly Chan and the Chinese businessmen backing the brothel.

Then on 8 November, 1994, a prostitute managed to escape from the building and phoned the other girls back at the house on the Bowery and begged them to call the police for help 'before it is too late'.

In the police raid that followed, Madam Lilly Chan was arrested, along with bouncer Joseph Morales and several others. Six more women turned themselves over to the authorities; the rest were set free.

Since then, the case has brought together more than a dozen defendants, from brokers in women to their buyers, and slowly unfolded the complex inner workings of the modern international slave trade.

Morales the bouncer was convicted of kidnapping

and civil rights violations. Ironically, Lilly Chan turned state's witness at Morales's trial and told the authorities cold-blooded details about how she oversaw that stable of sex slaves.

As Russ Bergeron of the United States immigration and Naturalization Service explained, 'The network was very sophisticated. These women were provided with false documents, false IDs, and they were even moved from city to city periodically in order to defeat law enforcement efforts.'

Many officials believe that there are numerous such slave brothels throughout the United States, many of them feeding off people's desperation to gain entry into the richest country in the world. 'It's almost in the nature of what we have seen in alien smuggling, because of the high cost for people coming in,' explained Daniel Moleno, the immigration agency's assistant district director for investigations, who helped supervise the raid on the Bowery brothel.

Happily, Na's tale ends well. After the immigration agency got working papers for her, she found a job at a Thai restaurant. Then one of her patrons fell in love with her and married her and she is planning to spend the rest of her life in America, where she hopes to raise a family.

12

Innocence for Sale

'This is a world of compensation; and he who would be no slave must consent to have no slave. Those who deny freedom to others deserve it not for themselves, and, under a just God, cannot long retain it.'

Abraham Lincoln, 1859

Wotganj Market, Calcutta, India, August, 1992.

A group of girls barely out of their teens play noisily by a gushing fire hydrant, their shrieks of laughter echoing round the squalid sidestreet as thousands of people pass through this busy thoroughfare.

One girl, dressed from head to toe in white cotton with two jet-black braids of hair tumbling down her front, stands out from the rest of the children in the middle of their game.

Saida is just thirteen years old, yet she has the demeanour of someone in their late teens, even early twenties. More than half a dozen bracelets dangle from her bony wrists. On her feet, neat gold sandals encase her carefully painted toe-nails.

Suddenly an older woman, called Anwari, standing by an abandoned shopfront beckons the child over to her. Saida moves dutifully away from her friends. None of them seem to notice or care as she breaks away and strides purposefully towards the older woman.

'All the young ones are virgins, we can guarantee that. The older ones will not be, they will have done some work,' comments Anwari to the man who is standing next to her on the edge of that busy marketplace.

These are the mean streets of Calcutta and anything goes if a man requires it. On this occasion, a well-dressed Arab is seeking an unblemished sexual partner, possibly as his wife. He turns to so-called Godmother Anwari while young Saida is still making her way towards them.

'How do you know she is a virgin?'

'We know,' comes the terse reply.

This is the ultimate human supermarket where people are sold like any other goods. There is even a choice of nationalities available — Chinese, Bangladeshi, Assamese, Tibetan and, of course, Indian. They are aged from ten upwards.

'Do you like what you see?' Godmother Anwari asks her prospective client wearily as the young Saida approaches.

'Hmmm. Yes. She looks perfect. How much?'

'$3,000 [£2,000],' replies Anwari, safe in the knowledge that she had paid $100 (£65) to the parents of these children for the right to sell them at the market.

'Too much. I'll give you $1,500 [£1,000].'

'No way. Forget it.'

Just then, Saida comes up to her Godmother and the man who is planning to bed her within hours and then turn her into his personal bride/sex slave.

'Show the gentleman your teeth, my dear.'

Saida bares her white, gleaming ivories.

'Very good,' says the Arab, without a trace of unease.

This strange trio then walks off towards the labyrinth of sidestreets to finalise negotiations away from any spying policemen who might not be willing to accept a bribe to ignore the sale of yet another human being at Watganj Market.

Eventually, Anwari succeeds in haggling the price up to $2,600 (£1,700) — this represents a very healthy profit on an initial outlay of no more than $100.

Just a few hours later, poor, innocent Saida is being subjected to the horrendous experience of losing her virginity at an age when most little girls are more interested in playing with dolls.

In some ways, though, she turns out to be one of the luckier ones. Her master is not as brutal as many of the men who purchase their own sex slaves with alarming regularity in this seedy, depressing market. At least she is not handcuffed to a bed each night to stop her escaping. At least she is well fed. At least her master buys her some new clothes.

'It could be much worse,' says Anwari.

But the fact remains that Saida is yet another lost innocent.

No one keeps written records of such unsavoury transactions but it is estimated that more than half of these child brides/slaves will die before they reach the ripe old age of 40. Abuse by their master/husband is the most common cause of death. However, many are just abandoned in the streets after a few years of sexual and physical abuse because it is so easy for men to find themselves replacement slaves.

In Saida's case, her apparently 'reasonable' master may eventually become abusive and then she will be lucky if she gets out alive. 'But what choice is there here for a young person?' says one local child welfare expert, 'They have little chance of a job. To some, the life of a slave/wife is far preferable to starving on the streets.'

Back on the streets near the chaotic market of Watganj, the talk is mostly of money. 'You want a virgin. I got just the girl,' insists a small Indian called Denis — greasy, sweaty and smelly, he is reminiscent of Dustin Hoffman in his most famous role in *Midnight Cowboy*. He does his deals on the move, and is 'shifty' in every sense of the word.

Suddenly, other hustlers appear beside us. They sense that a deal is going down and they want a chance to offer an ever better bargain.

'You want girl to keep? No problem.'

'Best girls. All virgins.'

'Young and clean. The only way.'

And so it goes on.

Meanwhile, dozens of other beady eyes lock on to anyone with apparent wealth.

The attraction of child brides/slaves is obvious. This is a country where most people earn about £3 a week. The chance to make a thumping profit will always take priority.

The slave girl network in Calcutta is a carefully orchestrated industry. Loose tongues can wreck the business overnight. It is an organised crime network where protection is absolutely essential. Godmothers like Anwari have at least two armed guards close by at all times, making sure that no one tries to rip them off or inform on them to the police. Often, Anwari finalises negotiations at the nearby Victorian Memorial Gardens, an open space with plenty of people wandering around.

Anwari soon forgets her 'godchild' Saida, who has now gone off with the Arab to her new life. Her latest concern is another customer whom she met earlier that day and has arranged to let him inspect more than a dozen prospective slave girls at the park.

This is when the true horror of this terrible business really hits home. Most of them are just innocent children, unaware of the horrors that await them in the outside world. Their fate is quite simple. Like Saida, they will probably be married to their suitor within hours of meeting him. Then, most probably, they will be put on a boat and shipped out of India rather than attract too much attention at the airport.

In 1991, a particularly horrific case was exposed when a 61-year-old Arab was arrested at Delhi airport, while taking an eleven-year-old girl back to the Middle East.

But the worst will occur when these innocent slave girls reach their final destinations. They will be sexually abused, raped and brutalised and, when they are finished with, either put to work scrubbing floors or divorced and thrown out. Many will simply 'disappear'.

There is not an ounce of feeling in Anwari's voice when she talks about her charges. She has been nurturing these innocents and their families since they were toddlers. 'They are healthy, beautiful creatures. Perfect for any man,' she says.

Now that they are old enough, she has even bought them fine saris so they look their best when sold. Those who are not 'lucky' enough to find a buyer will end up in a brothel.

Given the poverty of India, not to mention neighbouring Bangladesh, with few families able to afford the expensive dowries that daughters require if they are to be married off, there is a plentiful supply of little girls for unscrupulous women like Anwari.

She usually buys the little girls from their parents, who believe that their loved ones will be well cared for. Many of them are purchased for a minimal fee. Small wonder it is such a profitable business.

The girls themselves remain blissfully unaware of their fate. Their emotions have been, in many cases, virtually neutralised by years of non-parenting. They really have been bred to sell, just like cattle.

Meanwhile, the more perceptive of them are resigned to their fate. After all, they have had hard lives already, earning their keep by cleaning the brothels and cooking for the older prostitutes of the houses where they live.

'None of the girls can read or write,' says Anwari, without any note of surprise in her voice. 'They are all clean and virgins. I will guarantee that. They have never been touched by a man.'

Anwari asks the girls in front of prospective clients if they are virgins. They always nod their heads furiously. Anwari even assures customers that 'I have all the necessary paperwork and can take care of everything including the marriage.' Three-quarters of her fee, she explains to her male clients, is payable before the 'marriage' has taken place and the remainder is due immediately afterwards.

'I will not take less money because they have many years ahead of them to work in the brothels and that earns much money.'

Anwari discusses the details in much the same way as if she were selling chapattis or trinkets in the market. It just happens, in this case, to be the lives of little girls. The girls themselves find it difficult to relate to the fact that they might be about to be shipped out to a foreign country. It is confusing. Up until this point, most of their lives have been spent working as maids in a row of brothels in a market. The idea of travelling thousands of miles must be bewildering.

Some of them often enquire about travelling home to see their friends. Anwari answers them immediately: 'Of course you will.' To her mind, it is far preferable to deceive the girls than tell them the truth. 'It's better that way,' she insists.

On this particular occasion, in the safe, open space of the Memorial Park, Anwari's male client is uncertain about which of the girls he wants, so none of them is chosen. The girls go back to the playground and resume teasing one another like real children. Two pimps who have been watching the entire proceedings move away and eventually march over towards the play area.

The young girls immediately finish their game and start to follow their keepers. They are too young, too innocent and trusting to know the fate that awaits them ...

13

Jackie Who?

*'Slaves lose everything in their chains, even the desire
of escaping from them.'*

The Social Contract, Rousseau, 1762

2651 Walnut Grove, Rosemead, California, August,
1994.

Neighbours in this suburban, tree-lined street had
for some time been concerned by the activities at
number 2651, a two-storey, stucco-fronted, wood-
framed house rented out by its owner to a stunningly
attractive Asian woman known only as Jackie.

Jackie never had a problem coming up with the
monthly rent of just over $1,000 (£650), so nobody
really had any right to object to her presence in the area.
But some of the longer-term residents of this typically

suburban area near Los Angeles could not help noticing the constant flow of cars that pulled up in the driveway to the four-bedroom property.

'Jackie' Suphonphan Wood, 29 years old, with a penchant for designer-label outfits and weekly visits to the beauty parlour, was certainly a head-turner. She had the high cheek-bones that make Thai women classically beautiful and she had the confidence of someone ten years older.

But then Jackie had every right to look like a rich, successful businesswoman, because she was running a highly profitable industry importing female sex slaves from her home country. Her personal income was in excess of $200,000 (£130,000) a year.

Inside that immaculate residence were eight young Thai slave girls servicing up to thirty men a day between them. Their passports and money had been confiscated on arrival in California and they were paying off $30,000 (£20,000) 'debts' by each having to sleep with upwards of three hundred men.

Jackie made sure that there was a 24-hour guard at the house to prevent any of the girls escaping until their 'debts' had been fully paid off. There was Jackie's boyfriend, Tai Thahn Pham; Tom, a 20-year-old Vietnamese man; Jimmy, a 'security guard'; another slightly older Vietnamese man; as well as several other men holding similar positions.

To make matters worse, some of these men expected sex from the slave girls as part of their reward for keeping them imprisoned in the house. One of the guards was particularly brutal and all the women complained to Jackie about how he forced them to have sex.

Jackie did not really care. She was not paying the men huge salaries, so her main priority was to keep them happy, and if that meant allowing them to have free sex with the girls, then so be it.

One such girl was pretty, petite, dark-haired Anuthida. Her story is a classic example of how the lure of America has continued to prove the downfall of so many innocent people.

Anuthida, aged nineteen, met a Thai man called Luck in an office where she worked in Bangkok. 'You could make a lot of money in America. A pretty girl like you,' insisted Luck, a scrawny man in his late thirties.

'How?' asked innocent Anuthida.

'There are many good jobs in the States. I know many people there.'

'Really?' Anuthida said, not realising she was falling for the most obvious set-up in the world.

'I know one woman who runs a very successful business and she is always looking for new staff.'

Anuthida could not believe her luck. The very thought of working in America filled her with excitement. To most Thai girls, it was a dream that would never come true. But then she remembered how she had heard it was extremely difficult to get work visas. 'No problem. This woman I know guarantees you the job and then they issue the work visa,' Luck told her.

Luck had used the same lines on so many girls that he could reel them off automatically. But this one was even easier than usual. 'Give me a photo of yourself and I'll send it to this woman. If she likes the look of you, then we'll begin making the arrangements.'

'What arrangements?'

'Well, there's the airfare and the agency fee for arranging the job and work visa ...'

Within a few weeks, Anuthida had scraped together $1,000 (£650), consisting of her own hard-earned savings and a huge loan from her family. It was a down-payment to be paid back out of the wages from her new job, but it was obvious to everyone that this was a long-term investment.

The flight across the Pacific was the first time Anuthida had ever been out of her own country. She felt incredibly nervous flying to a strange land with strange people and no real friends of her own. But then she kept reminding herself that this was a great opportunity. Her friends and family had told her that she had to make the best of it because this might be the only chance she ever got.

At Los Angeles International Airport, Anuthida was met by a Thai man who did not even give her his name, but he did drive a big Chevrolet. It was the largest car Anuthida had ever ridden in, and its purring engine was worlds apart from the mopeds and tin heaps that filled the streets back home.

The man took Anuthida to a motel just a couple of miles from the airport where he said that the woman who was employing her would meet them. The man said little else during the journey, but Anuthida was too nervous to attach any significance to that. She was looking in wonder at the wide streets and huge houses all around her.

Anuthida was a little thrown when she found a note from her new boss in the hotel room, explaining that she could not get there until the next morning.

'You must stay here. She will collect you in the morning,' was all the driver told her.

Anuthida had a sleepless night. A combination of jet lag and the fear of being alone in a foreign land had made her feel a bit nervous about the entire adventure. For the first time, she began to wonder whether it was all as straightforward as she had presumed.

That night she tried to watch TV, but the vast choice of channels were in a language she could not understand. In any case, she just could not concentrate — the slightest noise outside her room frightened her. At least twice, Anuthida heard people's voices in other rooms and two men had a punch-up in the parking lot outside her door. Then, when she did finally get to sleep, an amorous couple in the next suite were having sex so noisily that the entire building seemed to shake.

Early next morning, there was a knock on the door. 'Hello, my name is Jackie,' said the attractive woman standing in front of Anuthida. As her eyes panned up and down Anuthida's body, Jackie purred 'You're even prettier in the flesh.'

Something about the way Jackie said this sent a shiver down Anuthida's spine, but she put her reaction down to exhaustion and her trepidation at arriving in a new place.

However, any fears she might have had soon disappeared when she saw Jackie's expensive car.

'She must be extremely successful,' thought poor, innocent Anuthida.

In the car, Jackie explained to her young recruit that her business was based in a quiet city called Rosemead, near Los Angeles. 'It's a very wealthy area.

There is little or no crime and the people are so civilised,' gushed Jackie to the overawed Anuthida.

As her car turned into the driveway of the house on Walnut Grove, the young Thai girl noticed a man hurrying out of the property and getting into a car which swiftly pulled away without even so much as acknowledging Jackie's arrival.

'Who was that?' asked Anuthida.

'Oh, that was a customer,' replied Jackie coolly.

Anuthida was immediately struck by the strange smell when she stepped inside the house A sickly sweet aroma wafted down the hallway from a number of rooms she could see at the end of a corridor. 'Come with me,' beckoned Jackie. Anuthida followed her new boss out into the back yard of the house where the sun was baking hot, but at least that awful smell was not so noticeable.

They sat at a garden table and Jackie opened a file. Inside, Anuthida could see that same photograph she had provided for Luck all those months ago in Bangkok. 'You're going to be a very successful girl for me,' said Jackie.

Just then, Anuthida noticed two skimpily clad Thai girls wandering through the house. An elderly man followed them and grabbed one of the girls from behind. Then they disappeared down a corridor.

'I expect you to go with at least three men a day,' said Jackie in a very matter-of-fact way.

'What?' replied Anuthida.

'Those are the terms if you are to repay the $30,000 [£20,000].'

Anuthida was momentarily confused — she tried

to piece together the evidence of the last few minutes: girls; men; strange aromas; money.

'This is a brothel?'

'What else d'you think it is?' snapped Jackie.

Suddenly, a tall, thin Vietnamese man called Tom appeared beside Jackie. 'Take her inside and show her around,' ordered Jackie.

'You can't make me do this. I'll go to the police.'

'Do that and you're dead,' came Jackie's icy response. Then she turned to Tom, 'Take her. NOW!' Anuthida was grabbed by the arm and pushed towards the French windows leading into the house.

'Don't worry my dear. You're a very pretty girl. All the men will want you and that debt will be paid off very quickly. You'll get a hundred dollars' credit for each customer you serve.'

That afternoon, Anuthida was forced to have sex with an old Asian man who was at least seventy years old. He smelt and he was very rough. That night, she cried herself to sleep in a single bed that she had to share with one of the other slave girls called Phanthila. They hardly exchanged a word before bedding down together. Jackie had warned the girls not to talk to each other. The punishment for breaking that rule was a severe beating followed by painful sex with one of the 'guards'.

The following morning, the girls were woken by Jackie at 6.30am and told to clean up the house in preparation for a busy day.

'We have at least a dozen customers booked in today. I want the place looking immaculate,' barked Jackie. Then she turned to Anuthida. 'You're coming with me.'

'Where?'

'Just get her in the car,' Jackie told Tom, the Vietnamese guard.

Jackie drove, with Tom sitting in the back of the car next to Anuthida just in case she tried to make a run for it. 'You would be foolish to try and leave us because we would find you,' said Jackie to her newest recruit as they pulled up outside a rundown building in a predominantly Asian area some ten miles from the house in Rosemead.

'What is this place?' asked Anuthida.

'You'll find out soon enough,' snapped Jackie.

They walked up to a back door to the building and Jackie knocked three times. An Asian man answered the door, looked around and then showed them inside the property. Jackie then pointed to a door. 'Go in there and wait for the doctor.'

'What?'

'Just do it.'

Anuthida went into the room. It was small, windowless and smelled musty. There was a medical trolley in the corner and one tatty-looking table lamp on the wooden floor.

Just then a short, fat, balding Asian man walked in wearing a tea-stained white doctor's coat. From a bag, he produced a syringe.

'What's going on?' asked a fearful Anuthida.

'Shut up, you whore.'

'But what are you going to do to me?'

'We're going to make sure you don't start breeding,' came the terse reply.

Within an hour, Anuthida had had a Norplant birth-control device implanted and was back in the car returning to Rosemead. This time she did not say a word to Jackie. Her fate was sealed. She was resigned to working as a sex slave. She tried to hold back the tears but it was impossible not to weep.

'Shut up,' said Jackie. 'You're in America, the land of opportunity.' She laughed.

For the following four months, Anuthida was expected to sleep with clients at whatever time of the day or night that Jackie demanded. The four other girls who worked at the house with her all seemed to have given up any desire to stay on in California once their so-called 'debt' to Jackie had been paid off. They all said they felt so battered by what had happened that they intended to return to Thailand as soon as they were released.

Unfortunately, Jackie had been entirely correct about one thing: Anuthida was immensely popular with the male customers because she was young and extremely attractive. Two of the other slave girls were very nasty towards Anuthida because they believed she was deliberately trying to lure customers away from them in an effort to pay off her 'debt' more quickiy than anyone else. But the truth was that Anuthida's innocence and beauty were proving a fatal attraction for many of the customers.

Jackie was delighted by Anuthida'a popularity because it meant that many men were using the services of her brothel more frequently than before. Sometimes, Jackie would force Anuthida to go with her to a hotel to meet richer clients, many of whom were Korean businessmen passing through California on some corporate trip or other.

At first, Anuthida refused to go with Jackie to a hotel on the basis that she would not be able to protect herself in the event that the client was expecting to do something 'too kinky'. Jackie was furious at Anuthida's defiance and ordered one of the bodyguards to handcuff her and march her back to the limo. It became clear to Anuthida that there was little point in resisting, even though she never accepted the fact that she was working as a prostitute.

To Anuthida's mind, she was a sex slave to an evil woman and her brigade of bullying bodyguards. She was being held against her will and had no choice but to sleep with hundreds of men. She would never have dreamt of becoming a prostitute if Jackie had not coerced her into it. Besides the obvious emotional turmoil caused by her captivity at the house, Anuthida found herself being subjected to numerous virtual rapes by men who believed that just because they were paying for sex it gave them the right to abuse her in this brutal fashion.

On a number of occasions, she was even forced to perform lesbian sex acts with the other girls at the house. Jackie warned her that if she did not cooperate, she would authorise her friends back in Thailand to attack Anuthida's family. Mistress Jackie also insisted on taking pornographic photos of Anuthida and the other girl with their customers, which she later threatened to send to her family if she stepped out of line.

At night, as she bedded down on one of the single beds that she shared with another girl, Anuthida found it particularly hard to sleep next to a girl she considered a friend, with whom she had been obliged to have sex only a few hours before.

Some days, Anuthida would look longingly out of the windows of the house at the children playing happily in the street, blissfully unaware of the tortuous regime that existed inside that neat-looking home. She began to wonder whether she would ever experience normal life again. She feared that Jackie would force her to stay on at the house even after her debt had been paid because she had proved so popular with the customers.

On Thursday, 22 September, 1994, Sergeant Tom Budds of the Asian Organised Crime Unit of the LAPD was informed that the FBI had uncovered a vast Thai sex slave racket that spread across the United States. The house on Walnut Grove was run as a brothel, insisted three informants who were helping the Californian authorities.

Within a week, Budds and his colleagues had gathered enough information to feel confident of a prosecution if they were to arrest Jackie and the others at the house.

So, on Friday, 30 September, Tom Budds obtained a search warrant from Whittier Municipal Court, signed by Judge Larry S Knupp, and headed for Rosemead accompanied by six other investigators, including personnel from the US Customs Department and the FBI. In a carefully planned operation, Budds and his team sent in Thai-speaking Agent Steve Tchen posing as a customer. When he knocked on the front door, Jackie appeared and was about to show Tchen in when Budds and his colleague Deputy Hugh Lloyd appeared in their official Sheriff's Department raid jackets to announce they had a search warrant.

Jackie tried to slam the door shut, but Budds got his foot in the door before she could do so and the team entered the premises at high speed. Within seconds they found a customer in the front room, two Thai slave girls in a downstairs bedroom, two more upstairs, another one in bed with a naked customer and another girl in the bathroom.

The girls were soon telling investigators that all-too-familiar horror story of how they had been trapped into becoming sex slaves for Jackie and her boyfriend, Tai Thahn Pham.

Over the following four hours, Budds and his team conducted interviews with all the subjects in the garage area of the house, while more than thirty customers continued to roll up to the property. Every client was detained and interviewed and admitted that the going rate for sex with one of the slaves was $100 (£65). It also emerged that the services provided by Jackie had been promoted mainly by word of mouth within the tightly knit Asian community of LA and the surrounding cities. Then, to his horror, Sergeant Tom Budds discovered that Jackie and her bodyguards kept a large Taser gun in the front living room — it had been used to intimidate troublesome girls.

The house itself was sparsely furnished, with just one couch in the living room and a thin mattress on the floor of each of the bedrooms, plus a few closets with the girls' clothes in them. Numerous other pieces of evidence were recovered from the house by the investigators, and Jackie Wood rapidly confessed to her role in the sex slave racket.

Another disturbing element emerged when it was revealed that two other slave girls had escaped from the house in Rosemead just two days before the raid and were being pursued by a 'hit team' from Thailand, determined to take revenge on the girls for daring to run away. The girls have never been located and it is feared that they may have been killed.

On 3 October, felony charges were filed against Jackie Wood and her lover, Pham. These included four counts each of pimping and pandering with a possible prison sentence of thirty-two years. Wood was also charged with peonage (slavery) violation, which could bring a prison sentence of between two and ten years.

Meanwhile, the slave girls found inside the Rosemead house were held in protective custody to prevent any of Wood's associates from intimidating them before the trial.

Additional charges of several counts of rape were made against Jackie Wood and Pham for having forced the girls to engage in sex. They faced life imprisonment if found guilty of those charges.

In January, 1995, both Wood and Pham pleaded guilty to pimping, pandering and false imprisonment. Pham was sentenced to three years in prison while Woods got four years. The pair pleaded guilty rather than face a trial and sentences of up to thirty years in prison if found guilty on all counts. As part of the deal, Pham and Wood also gave the authorities information that may help track an organised crime operation believed to stretch from Asia to the western United

States.

The authorities — who characterised the case as 'slave trade 1990s-style' — also revealed that the women imprisoned in the house were to be transported back to Thailand by the US Immigration and Naturalization Service.

14

The Marriage 'Contract'

'All spirits are enslaved, which serve things evil.'
Shelley, 1818

Whitburn, West Lothian, Scotland, October, 1992.

Joy Johnson was feeling bored and restless in this tiny mining community. At 24 years of age, a trim brunette, she felt she had the potential to land a good job, but the opportunities were few and far between in a place like Whitburn.

So, when one of her girlfriends called up and said she was travelling down to London and would Joy like to accompany her, she leapt at the opportunity, especially when her friend Kirsty said something about earning some money.

On the train south, Kirsty revealed to Joy an extraordinary story about how she was actually travelling to London to take part in an arranged marriage for which she was going to get the not inconsiderable sum of £1,000. 'I could probably get you a hubby,' laughed Kirsty.

'For that kind of money, I'd marry Frankenstein,' said Joy.

Within a day of arriving in London, Joy had been promised £800 if she would marry a Polish waiter, enabling him to continue to live in Britain legally. 'It seemed like easy money and I couldn't see any harm in it at the time,' explained Joy later.

In London, she and Kirsty stayed with a woman called Kim at her house in the centre of the city. 'For a couple of days we had a great time travelling around London and seeing the sights.'

Kirsty 'married' another Pole, a student, at Westminster Register Office with Kim acting as witness. Joy was due to do likewise a few days later. Then one evening, Kim introduced Kirsty and Joy to a sharp-suited character who proudly and openly boasted that he was a pimp.

'He came over to Kim's place and brought a whole load of drugs and we got completely loaded,' explained Joy. 'I could hardly stand up by the end of the evening.'

The young Scottish girl then made the mistake of sleeping with the pimp — and that was when her problems began. Her friend Kirsty had gone off with friends.

In the middle of the night, she stirred from her drug-induced slumber to find her hands bound together with a tie.

'I was terrified and started shouting and screaming for Kim, but the house was empty,' recalled Joy.

After struggling to get off the bed, she discovered to her horror that the doors were double locked and she was trapped inside the house. Joy was distraught. She fell back on to the bed with her wrists still manacled and cried herself to sleep.

At noon the next day, the pimp reappeared at the house and Joy pleaded with him to release her.

'I started crying with desperation. Then he punched me in the face and called me a Scotch cow.'

Joy fell over and lay on the floor with her wrists still tied. The man grabbed her by the waist and forced her over on to her stomach. 'Bitch. Fucking bitch,' he muttered under his breath as he ripped down her panties and then unzipped his fly. After satisfying his lust, the pimp told Joy how sorry he was for being aggressive.

'If you're so sorry, why am I still tied up?,' screamed Joy, still in pain following his brutal attack. The pimp bent over her and untied her wrists.

'I said I was sorry and I meant it,' said the man as he struggled to undo the tight knot.

Joy felt an overwhelming sense of relief at her 'release'. She tried to remain calm, although her feisty Scottish character made her want to be very aggressive towards the pimp.

For the next few minutes, they eyed each other uncomfortably as Joy tried to gather up her things so that she could move permanently out of that house. Then the pimp caught her eye and she could have sworn he had another smirk on his face.

'You fucking hate me, don't you?' he said.

'D'you blame me?' replied Joy, whose pride was such that she could not resist fighting back. She regretted her comment the moment she saw the expression on his face. It was almost identical to the way he had looked before he had raped her earlier. He grabbed her. She struggled but could sense that the more she fought back, the more he would hurt her.

This time he tied her ankles tightly together and pushed her face down on the smelly mattress in the corner of the room. At first, Joy tried to kick out to stop him but each time she kicked him, he retaliated with a crunching fist in her kidneys. Then he dragged her off the mattress by her hair and started to smash her head on the wooden floor. She realised then that to resist was madness.

The next moment, he was forcing her mouth open with his fingers. She dreaded what he was about to do to her. She feared the worst. He poked one finger so far down her throat that she almost vomited. Then she felt some kind of tablet being put into her mouth.

'Swallow it, you bitch. NOW!' he screamed at her. Joy had no choice. She wanted to spit it out but knew that he would beat her senseless if she did not obey his command. She rapidly lost her sense of balance and then became vaguely aware of him starting to have sex with her once again.

Not long afterwards, Joy Johnson passed out.

She woke up next morning covered in deep, dark bruises and with congealed blood hanging from her nose from where he had attacked her.

'Get up,' barked the pimp within seconds of Joy

opening her eyes. 'I've got work for you.'

He threw her clothes on to the mattress next to her.

'Hurry up. I've got a cab waiting outside.'

'Fuck off,' Joy screamed back at the pimp.

'Shut up, bitch. You're mine until you wed that Polish guy next week. I own you. Try to run away and I'll come after you.'

For the first time, it dawned on Joy that she was completely trapped. He was her slave master and she knew that he meant every word he said.

Less than half an hour later, she was bundled out of a taxi by the pimp and into a rundown house filled with shabby bedsit flats. At the top of three flights of creaking stairs they came to a door. 'Open up, Bob, it's me. I've got you a prezzie,' shouted the pimp.

The door swung open and Bob stood there, well over 50 years old, a vast beer gut hanging over the top of his trousers and greasy, matted hair combed forward to hide his balding pate.

His eyes roved up and down Joy's body and he licked his sweaty lips.

'I owe you one, mate,' said Bob as he grabbed Joy by the hand and pulled her inside the bedsit, leaving the pimp outside.

'Come with me,' he said, his clammy hand clutching her by the wrist as he led her to a filthy looking double bed in the far corner of the room.

'Get your clothes off, love,' said Bob. 'I've got a few little surprises for you.'

He pulled open the top drawer of a cheap-looking chest and pulled something out. Joy did not look up, but she had a horrible feeling she knew what he was doing.

Bob threw a dildo on to the bed and it landed with a thud right next to Joy.

'Pick it up and use it on yourself,' he told her quietly, but firmly. 'I can do what the fuck I want with you for the next hour or two.'

After more than an hour of vile sex, Bob started complaining to Joy that she was not satisfying him properly. Joy — still high from the tablet that the pimp had forced down her earlier — could barely focus on the animal that was molesting her.

Suddenly, out of nowhere, she felt Bob's fist crunch into her face, opening up the wound earlier inflicted by the pimp. Joy virtually lost consciousness when his fist connected, she lost her balance and fell off the bed, hitting her head on the floor as she keeled over. When she came round a few hours later, Bob had gone but her pimp was back.

He told her that he had plenty more like Bob. 'And if you give me any aggro, I'll fucking kill you.'

'But why are you doing this?'

'You're gonna make me some cash if it's the last thing you do. '

The pimp then informed Joy that her bogus marriage had been delayed for two weeks and that she would be his sex slave untill the wedding.

Over the following fourteen days, she was forced to sleep with more than a dozen men. 'I was his sex slave. I had no choice, I could not escape because I genuinely feared he would hunt me down and kill me,' she recalled many months later.

Many of the pimp's customers insisted on performing unnatural sex acts on Joy and at least five of them demanded bondage sessions during which she was tied up and whipped or beaten. On the night before her bogus marriage ceremony, she could not sleep because of the pain inflicted on her by the animals she had been forced to sleep with.

Somehow, the pimp kept his word and released Joy in time for her to go through with her fake marriage to a Pole called Jacek at Haringey Register Office, in north London.

She fled back to Scotland within hours of the ceremony, fearful that the pimp might change his mind and come after her. She never spoke to Kirsty again or ever dared to return to London.

15

A Madam for All Seasons

'Slaves cannot breathe in England, if their lungs
Receive our air, that moment they are free;
They touch our country and their shackles fall.'

The Task, *William Cowper, 1743-1809*

Apartment Block, Central London, October, 1995.

With her wire-framed spectacles, a penchant for expensive powersuits with huge shoulder pads and a £1,000 wrist-watch, Nathsuda looks more like a well-heeled businesswoman than a slave girl trader — but then that is because she is making a fortune out of forcing innocent young women to sell their bodies.

Nathsuda — or Maria, as she prefers to be called by her clients — is proud of her 'business' and the human cargo she deals in. She rules her girls with iron discipline.

Her apartment, in one of London's most exclusive areas, always has at least three pretty young slave girls ready and waiting for any one of her hundreds of male and female customers.

Maria, aged 42, prefers to offer teenage girls for sex because many of her clients like them to pretend they are schoolgirls. The younger women are also much easier for Maria to intimidate if they try to escape.

In the one-year period up to October, 1995, Maria took delivery of seventeen slave girls from provinces of some of the poorest countries in South East Asia.

They are lured to London with the promise of reasonably paid secretarial jobs, only to arrive and have their passports confiscated by 'new boss' Maria, who also employs English women as 'maids' to keep an eye on them and make sure they do as she commands.

Maria also 'sub-lets' some of the more trusted girls out to other escort agencies and massage parlours in London knowing full well that they will not try to escape because she has retained their travel documents. 'Each girl costs me about £10,000 and my people in Thailand make all the arrangements and will deliver them to any address you want in Britain. When they arrive, I get a phonecall and collect them from whatever hotel they're waiting in. An escort brings them over to make sure they get through immigration without any hassles. There haven't been any problems so far because the visas are genuine. They have got someone inside the embassies to fix that for them.'

The girls are supplied to Maria on bizarre six-month contracts which she devised because 'most of them run out of steam after that period of time, so it is better to get replacements.

'Because of my investment, I have to keep them under proper control and make sure they work efficiently,' she says, 'By not staying any longer than six months they don't even have time to make friends, which is perfect.

'I don't want them running off before the contract has finished. They're here to make me money.'

Maria personally trains the girls on their arrival in Britain. As a former sex slave herself, she says she knows all the tricks. 'They have to give a man pleasure or he will not want to come back, and repeat business is the key to this trade.'

Maria — who admits to being bisexual — even 'breaks in' some of her favourite girls herself and insists, 'Sure, I own them and I guess they are slaves, but I tell them to just get on with it because they won't be with me for that long.'

Until only two years ago, Maria herself worked at a sex sauna in east London.

Maria is netting thousands of pounds a week from her slave girl racket, which services at least ten men every day at the well-appointed apartment she rents near Marble Arch, just a stone's throw from the Queen's home at Buckingham Palace.

Maria's sordid business attracts many customers through advertising cards distributed in telephone kiosks in London's West End. She promotes the girls as 'beautiful new Japanese students'.

If they are lucky, the girls who work for Maria receive a small pay-off at the end of their six-month stint in London.

But the fact remains that they are effectively slaves because they are not free to leave her sordid business.

As one girl said, 'We come to England expecting a proper job and then get told we have no choice but to work as prostitutes. It is degrading and depressing and we are definitely slaves. There is no other word for it.'

The slave girl network that supplies women to mistresses like Maria is worth revealing in more detail because these so-called 'agents' are reckoned to be supplying sex slaves to the United States, Japan, Malaysia and Singapore, as well as to numerous other European countries, besides Britain.

The racket is backed by organisations like the Thai mafia and the girls know that any attempt to escape will provoke violent retaliation against their families back home. One of the 'slave lords' in Thailand is 42-year-old Rivi Suenkanokpan, who is known as the 'Fat Man' to clients like Mistress Maria. He owns a business exporting bamboo chopsticks and toothpicks.

The Fat Man and his wife run their lucrative vice sideline from their home near Bangkok Airport. He frequently travels to capital cities like London, Washington and Tokyo to escort recruits to their new vice bosses.

Every visit has been immensely succcessful. At London's Heathrow Airport, for example, the girls are always waved straight through after the immigration officer stamps the date of entry on their passports. 'I go with them to answer any awkward questions,' he says.

The Fat Man claims that getting visas at the British

Embassy in Bangkok is 'very easy'. He went on, 'It's actually easier than finding good-quality girls!

'The girls have no money, so we fake job references and details of bank accounts, so everything looks official. We don't need any money up front.

'The clients pay cash on delivery when the girls arrive in England with their suitcases.'

The Fat Man insisted that he has 'girls on tap' whom he could persuade into going abroad at a few day's notice. 'They think it's the beginning of a dream existence in a new country. They never question us closely about the type of job that might be available. They are that desperate.'

The slave girls themselves often turn out to be naive women who have never been outside their own village.

But the Fat Man is always on the lookout for a particular type of girl — virgins. He claims they are worth at least a third more to clients like Mistress Maria He boasts that one attractive sixteen-year-old virgin was sold on to three consecutive mistresses, each time at a profit, until she was finally bought by an Arab client who flew her to his home in the Middle East where he imprisoned her for seven months.

The Fat Man's team in Thailand consists of a bizarre group of criminals whose duties read like an extract from a novel: Sam procures gullible girls from the provinces; Laddawan hides them in safe houses while their travel documents are being prepared; then a master forger called Moo provides much of the false documentation.

Back in London, one of the girls who was forced into prostitution by the unscrupulous Maria revealed how she was kept trapped in a sordid cycle of sexual depravity. 'I was tricked into travelling to London and then forced by Maria to be a hooker. Maria promised that it would all turn out OK because I would earn enough money to go home and buy my parents a house,' explained slave girl Mai. 'But Maria took all the money directly off the clients and never gave any of it to me. When I threatened to go, she raped me with a sex toy and then tied me to a chair for two days.'

Mai, nineteen, says that she then realised she could not escape from Maria's clutches 'because she knew where my family were and threatened to have them killed if I tried to make a run for it.'

Mai, from one of the poorest regions of South Vietnam, then disclosed some of the appalling sex acts she was forced to perform for some of Maria's perverted clients.

'One time, Maria got me to go to this Japanese businessman's house in Belgravia with another of her girls called Ari,' explained Mai.

'When we got there, we found that he had invited seven male friends round to the house and he expected us to sleep with all of them.

'When I refused, he and two of the other men got very nasty and beat me while two of the others raped the other girl.

'Then they raped me and beat her. It was horrible. Then, when they finished, instead of letting us go they locked us in a room together and insisted we sleep with each other while they took it in turns to watch us through the keyhole.

'At first, we halfheartedly kissed and cuddled on the bed. Then the host burst into the room and started beating us both with a horsewhip because he said we were not doing it properly.

'Then we had to promise to have full sex with each other. It was disgusting. We could hear them breathing and moaning outside the door as they watched. They even left the phone off the hook so some of them could listen on an extension.

'Every now and again, one of them would shout obscenities at us through the door. They even made us talk dirty to each other so they could hear.'

But Mai and Ari's ordeal did not end there.

Mai went on, 'After more than an hour trapped in that room, all eight of the men came in and raped us in turn. We held hands throughout and shut our eyes and tried not to think about what was happening. But I will never forget it as long as I live.'

Mai finally escaped from Maria's evil clutches by pretending her mother back in Vietnam was dying from cancer. The sadistic mistress uncharacteristically took pity on the young girl and allowed her to leave.

'Maria used to always say she fancied me and I am certain she had a soft spot for me. I think that's why she let me go.'

Others have not been so lucky.

Ari finally left Maria after six months, penniless and badly beaten after rowing with her mistress. She was so desperate to survive, she had to work as a street hooker. She has not had a normal job since.

'Not only does Maria turn us into sex slaves, but

she effectively ruins most of our lives for ever. She is the sickest woman I have ever met,' added Mai.

The police have so far failed to gather enough evidence in this case to feel confident of bringing a successful prosecution.

16

Behind Closed Doors

'There is no doubt that slavery is taking place in England. Who would have thought that such a state of affairs is possible?'

Lord Longford, Speaking In Britain's House of Lords, 28 November, 1990

Bexley Heath, Kent, England, Autumn, 1990.

Leafy, suburban streets dominate this town on the edge of south London. Homes tend to be semi-detached. Gardens are always immaculately groomed, with neatly clipped privet hedges and well-mowed lawns. There is also a proliferation of net curtains in front windows — perfect for nosy neighbours to keep an eye on their fellow residents.

Bexley Heath is certainly the last place you would expect to find a slave girl ...

Dr Truman Abassah, a respected surgeon at south London's Brook Hospital, and his wife, a personnel officer with Greenwich Health Authority seemed, on the surface, to be the sort of residents that towns like Bexley Heath thrive on: middle-class, reserved and very, very polite. There were never any parties or loud music at the Abassahs' spacious, four-bedroom house — they never caused any trouble.

But behind the closed doors of that comfortable house all kinds of terrors were being inflicted in the name of domestic servitude. For Dr Abassah and his wife, Philomena, had a propensity for sadistic violence when it came to dealing with their maid, Helen Samuels.

And on one particular afternoon, Mrs Abassah had a particularly twisted motive for attacking her servant: she believed the girl was having an affair with her husband. 'I know you've been to bed with him. I know,' muttered Philomena to the bemused and terrified 25-year-old Helen. The young woman had endured almost four years of torture, beatings, starvation and neglect at the hands of her master and mistress, but this latest development had shocked her.

A few minutes earlier, Philomena had arrived home unexpectedly early from work to find Helen sitting in the kitchen. That, alone, had sparked a mini-explosion because Helen was usually locked outside when the couple went off to work in the morning. They had told their slave girl that they did not trust her in the house on her own.

Helen had discovered a spare key some months earlier and would slip into the house after her mistress had departed, always making sure she was back outside in the yard by the time Philomena returned.

'Never. Never come inside this house again when I am not here. Do you understand, girl?' Philomena bellowed at the poor creature.

That was when she had thrown in this extraordinary accusation about Helen having an affair with Dr Abassah. Well, it was ludicrous from Helen's point of view because she loathed him as much as she hated Philomena. But the problem was that she had been enduring regular sexual harassment from the good doctor since her arrival at the household.

It started with wandering hands and had progressed to the point where Dr Abassah would deliberately ensure he could catch Helen alone at least once a week for some sickening self-gratification.

'If you lay another finger on him, I'll kill you,' screamed Philomena at her silent servant. 'I know he's in love with you.'

Philomena then took a long breath, almost as if she was trying to convince herself before she continued, 'I've seen the way he looks at you. I know the signs. It's not the first time, you know.'

Philomena was not looking for a response from Helen. She had long since forbidden her maid from talking back to her unless asked a specific question. She just enjoyed hearing the sound of her own voice.

'I've never trusted you. I think you want him all to yourself. Well, you're not going to get him ...

She stopped mid-sentence. The front door slammed shut and put a sudden stop to her tirade. The good doctor was home.

Dr Abassah was neat, bespectacled and rotund, with a fondness for three-piece suits even on the hottest summer day. He had that typical doctor's habit of bringing his bedside manner home with him and would evade potential problems at home by always replying to his wife's outbursts with the sweetest, 'Oh, you're absolutely right, my darling.'

As he walked into the kitchen that day, he undoubtedly sensed the tension in the air, but then that was nothing knew inside the Abassah household. Violence ruled.

The doctor greeted his wife fondly and swiftly retreated to his upstairs office. This was one argument he had the good sense to keep out of.

Philomena continued, screaming 'I've seen the way he looks at you. Pure lust, and you are encouraging him. Touch him again and you're dead.'

Poor Helen stood there, shaking. She was too scared to respond. She knew that her mistress was spoiling for a fight and it would be a battle that only Philomena could win.

But Helen's silence only fuelled Philomena's rage. She was literally grinding her teeth with fury. She stared manically at her servant.

'Get out! Don't come back until the morning,' she screamed.

Helen moved off towards the back door to the garden and the paving slab that had become her cold and miserable night-time retreat.

Suddenly, Philomena lunged at Helen, forcing her to the ground. Then she straddled the girl, who was lying face down, and began to squeeze her round the neck. Her nails were digging deep into Helen's flesh and the pain was excruciating. Then Helen started to lose her breath. 'Bitch. I know. I know ...'

At that moment, Dr Abassah appeared in the kitchen looking completely unconcerned that his wife was on the floor throttling the maid. He said nothing and just moved quietly across the room to a cabinet where he took out a glass and then poured himself some milk.

He glanced down at the attempted murder only two feet away and flashed a brief, greasy smile.

'Darling, do we have any biscuits anywhere?'

Philomena paused midway through strangling Helen.

'Try the pantry.'

Dr Abassah shuffled off and Philomena decided to halt her latest attempt to kill Helen. She stood up, brushed down her dress and did not utter a word to her maid. Helen rushed for the back door. The near freezing temperatures outside were far preferable to what was happening inside that terrible house.

It had not always been so awful at the Abassahs. When Helen first started working for them in 1985, the couple simply ignored their maid, even though she was actually a distant relative.

Helen had first encountered her new master and mistress when she was living at home in Nigeria. Her aunt was Mrs Abassah's stepmother and when Philomena suggested she might like to join her and her husband in England, Helen leapt at the chance.

But within weeks of arriving in Britain, strange things started to happen. To begin with, Helen — whose mother had died many years previously — only received one letter from her family back home. It came from her brother, warning her never to return to Nigeria because her aunt had been so upset at her decision to leave and work for the Abassahs that she had disowned her.

Unfortunately, Helen's master and mistress were not in the slightest bit interested in her family problems. They shouted at her and insisted she work morning, noon and night. But at least she had a roof over her head and a means of survival.

But then one day Philomena started shouting at Helen about the dirty kitchen floor. She grew angrier and angrier. That was when she hit Helen for the first time.

A couple of days later, she gave her a severe thrashing with a stick because she did not like the way Helen had stacked the clean dishes.

Helen thought about running away, but she had no friends and nowhere to go. Once, she got as far as the nearest railway station, only to turn back when she realised she did not even have enough cash to pay for a ticket to London.

When she got home, the doctor and his wife were waiting for her.

'How dare you leave this house without my permission,' said Abassah in a cold, steely voice. His wife looked on with a smug grin on her face. She knew what was coming next.

'Come here, girl,' beckoned the doctor. His breathing quickened. 'Bend over the table. I'm going to teach you some manners.'

Helen closed her eyes and tried to think about something else. She felt his hand grab her flesh and squeeze. What was happening?

Just then the doctor crashed the palm of his hand across her backside. Then he grabbed a book from the table next to her and started smashing it across the backs of her thighs.

Helen opened her eyes slightly and looked across the room at Philomena. She was smirking, clearly enjoying every moment of her husband's brutality.

Within a few months of that first attack, Helen had become so used to the beatings inflicted on her by the doctor and his wife that she would feel relieved if he only used his fists rather than an actual weapon.

Then one day, the doctor exploded in anger at Helen because she could not find his slippers. After the customary spanking on her backside, Abassah insisted that his slave should lie on her back on the floor of the living room. A shiver of fear went through Helen's body.

'Don't move, girl,' barked the doctor.

Then he opened the drawer of a nearby bureau and took something out. It was a large safety-pin.

Helen started shaking even more violently.

'Don't move,' repeated the doctor, as if he was about to inject a patient with medicine.

Just then, Helen felt a sharp, stabbing sensation in her side. Then another in her shoulder. Then another in her breast. He was stabbing her frenziedly with the safety-pin — she felt short, sharp pains all over her body. Ten minutes later he stopped, having inflicted at least a hundred tiny wounds, leaving speckles of blood on Helen's T-shirt and jeans. Terrified, she ran from the room.

During another beating, Helen was hit on the

head with a tray by Philomena until fragments of it were embedded in her scalp. 'You're bleeding on the carpet. Get out!' screamed Philomena hysterically, following that crazed attack.

Helen later recalled, 'I went to the bathroom to bathe my head and put my face right into the water. It was dark red with my blood.'

Dr and Mrs Abassah then began a new regime of starving Helen into submission. Before leaving for work, they would check all the food in their house.

'If I touched the food, I would get a beating when they came home,' explained Helen later. 'I began to eat apples and pears from the garden, although they were often unripe.'

And when the Abassahs did give their slave girl anything to eat, it would invariably be past its sell-by date. 'I remember Philomena telling me to drink milk that was sour. It was watery and there were lumps in it.'
As a further punishment, Helen was regularly forced to wash her mouth out with water containing sterilising tablets.

By this time, Helen weighed less than seven stone and hardly an inch of her body was unmarked from the beatings. She was also forced to sleep outside the back door, mainly because Philomena was growing so paranoid about her husband having an affair with the slave girl.

One day, Helen was so hungry that she left a begging note for the next-door neighbours, Doris and Reg Tapley. It read, 'Please help me by leaving bread or biscuits by your door.'

It was Helen's first message to the outside world.

The Tapleys were understandably shocked by the situation. They had heard a few crying sounds coming from the house but never frequently enough to warrant any investigation.

However, when they noticed that Helen was sleeping outside, the Tapleys alerted the police and the Abassahs were arrested.

Dr Abassah and his wife, Philomena, were jailed for five years for torturing and starving Helen Samuels. They were also ordered to be deported back to Nigeria after they had completed their sentences.

Judge Jonathan Van Der Werff said it was difficult to understand how a doctor could have inflicted such suffering on a young girl. The court heard that Helen had worked at least thirteen hours a day, seven days a week and had never received a penny in wages.

Her rescuers, Doris and Reg Tapley, became Helen's close friends after her release from captivity. Mrs Tapley said, 'I really hope they give her a fair chance, especially if they consider what she's been through.

'Anyone who saw her when she was taken away by the police would have felt as sick as I did. I feel Helen is very lucky to be alive.'

Helen herself said that life with the Abassahs 'made me wish I was dead'. She added, 'I cannot forgive them.' Detective Constable Stephen Westwood said the case was 'shocking', adding, 'I've never seen anything like this before. I was horrified and couldn't believe it could happen in this country.'

Helen has now recovered sufficiently from her ordeal to start a new life in south London where she has been attending dressmaking classes at college.

She says simply, 'I did whatever the Abassahs said because I was frightened for my life. I used to lie awake at night and pray, saying to God, "If this is the way you want it, I'll put up with it. But if it isn't, then please, please make it stop." '

17

Vice Trap

'Crime and punishment grow out of one stem.'
Emerson, 1841

Marbella, Costa Del Sol, Spain, July, 1995.

For more than ten years, British girls have been lured into a life of vice in this immensely popular resort area. All too often, naive youngsters fly out to the sunshine coast looking for fun, adventure and romance; many hope to settle down to a glamorous lifestyle and a glittering career a million miles away from the dole queues and freezing temperatures back in Britain.

But for one such girl, those dreams fell cruelly apart when she became ensnared in a den of depravity from which there was no escape. This is her story ...

Paula O'Neill's decision to turn her life around and move to the Costa del Sol was greeted with complete indifference by her family in the British town of Luton, Bedfordshire, just north of London.

'Why don't you get a proper job?' asked her father, when Paula, aged 22, announced she had been hired by a time-share company to sell apartments on a complex near Marbella.

'That's boring, Dad. I want some adventure,' replied Paula. She meant every word. However, within two weeks of arriving in Spain, she started to regret that bold statement.

For her job selling shares in apartments entailed considerably more persuasion of clients than Paula had ever imagined. Some of the other girls she met at the complex on the first day of her new job even suggested that the only way to make a quick sale and earn some hefty commission was to sleep with prospective male clientèle.

Paula was appalled at the prospect and after fruitlessly trying to prove her point by getting a 'straight' sale without any sexual enticement, she quit in disgust. The problem was that the job had come with a free apartment and that meant she was out on the streets with only a few hundred pounds in savings and a handful of phone numbers of friends.

Paula's pride prevented her from returning home. She had a point to prove to her folks and she was determined not to give up at the first hurdle. She checked into a cheap hotel and started looking for work. It was not as easy as she had expected. She spoke no

Spanish and there had been a recent backlash against the British in the area, which had resulted in a spirit of non-cooperation when it came to locals employing anyone English.

One night — down on her luck and feeling very sorry for herself — Paula arranged to meet a girlfriend from the time-share business for a drink at the picturesque port area on the edge of Marbella.

It was a steaming hot evening and thousands of revellers were packing the narrow streets, pouring in and out of the numerous bars, clubs and casinos. Paula's friend never showed up that night, but she enjoyed a few drinks, got chatting to a charming Arab from one of the yachts moored in the harbour and tried to forget all about her troubles.

By midnight, Paula and her new friend, who called himself Ali, had been joined by a couple of other English girls. Paula found them a little too forward for her liking. She suspected that they might have been high-class hookers, many of whom wandered in and out of the bars in the port looking for rich clients.

With the sangria flowing and everyone in high spirits, Paula did not object when Ali suggested that all the girls might like to come aboard his yacht for a nightcap. What could possibly happen, she wondered. There were three of them against one man, after all.

As the party stumbled up the gangplank of the vast 120-foot yacht with its whirling radar scanner, Paula remembers taking off her black stilettos because the heels kept getting stuck in the wooden ridges on the deck.

She cannot remember anything after that until she woke up the next morning to find herself tied to a bed and stripped of her clothes. Something was covering her mouth as well.

'I thought I was dreaming. I shut my eyes tightly and then opened them slowly. But I was still there,' she recalled later. 'There was a rocking sensation and I realised I was still on the yacht and it was out at sea.'

Just then, two men walked into the room. Paula shut her eyes and listened. One of them was the man who called himself Ali, but the other was an older Arab in a head-dress and flowing white robes. He looked at least 60 years of age.

Paula opened her eyes just wide enough to sneak a glance at them. She prayed they would think she was still unconscious, because she needed time to think what to do.

They were speaking in Arabic and the conversation was very heated. Suddenly, the older man started prodding Ali in the shoulder angrily. Ali then stormed out of the room. The man walked towards her, smiling.

'You're awake,' he said pointedly.

Paula did not stir in the hope he would go away. But she knew he knew she was pretending.

He sat on the edge of bed and ran a hand slowly up the inside of her thigh. Paula could feel her flesh crawling.

'Wake up. It's time,' said the old Arab. His hand stopped at the top of her thigh. Then he pinched her roughly.

Paula's eyes snapped open angrily. He smiled.

She tried to move but the ropes around her wrists and ankles stung painfully as they tightened. His hand moved to her face and he ran a finger across her lips. It tickled in a nasty kind of way. Paula started hyperventilating as a direct result of her fear and embarrassment. She could not talk because a black silk scarf was gagging her.

'You're beautiful,' he muttered, as his eyes scanned her body. Then Paula really started struggling. She wanted him to know she was not about to give up her body without a fight. But she also felt horribly vulnerable, lying there naked.

He undid the gag.

Paula spluttered, gasping for breath. 'You bastard. Let me go.' She spat the words out contemptuously. He seemed even happier at her outburst.

'You English girls are so spirited.'

He bent down and tried to kiss her on the lips. She bit him hard. He reacted furiously and hit her across the face with the back of his hand.

'Now, it's time ...'

Three hours later, the old Arab finally left the room. Paula's entire face was horribly bitten and bruised. She was crying. Then Ali entered.

'I am sorry if he was rough with you but that is his way ...'

'Let me go, you bastard!' she screamed through her tears.

'I cannot do that yet. He wants you to stay for a few days.'

'I'd rather die,' Paula told Ali defiantly.

He then sat down on the end of the bed and admitted that her drinks had been drugged that night in the bar and she was basically their prisoner. 'You'll survive this if you cooperate. We pay very generously.'

'Fuck your money and fuck you. Just drop me at

the nearest port,' said Paula, but she knew that would not happen. She was being held captive and they could do whatever they liked to her.

Later that day, the older Arab returned and carried on where he had left off earlier. Paula turned her head to one side and prayed that it would soon end.

Paula O'Neill's ordeal went on for three more agonising days. At times she felt like fighting back, but she eventually became resigned to her fate, realising that it was probably the key to her survival.

Eventually, the old Arab grew bored of her and she was dropped back at Marbella port. Ali gave her £5,000. At first, she tried to throw it back at him.

But then he said, 'Take it. It'll help you survive. It's tough out here.'

'I'm not a hooker. I don't do it for money.'

'That's not the point,' said Ali. 'If you want to avoid being taken prisoner again, you should take the money.'

Paula hated herself for it, but she kept the cash.

She went back to her hotel, showered, cried, ate and then cried again.

'I hated myself even more than I hated them. But I had to survive.'

Within two months of her sex slave ordeal, Paula became a full-time call-girl on the Costa del Sol. After all that fighting, she had given up the battle.

'One night I bumped into those same girls who were with me when Ali drugged my drink. They introduced me to a madam, called Candy, in a bar.

'She said I could earn a fortune because English girls were in big demand — especially with Arabs.'

Candy helped set Paula up in a rented apartment with three other girls in the centre of Marbella. 'It's strange the way things have turned out. Those three or four days on the yacht were a living nightmare I shall never forget, yet my experiences numbed me to everything else.

'I just don't think about the same sort of things anymore. I have a life to live. It's not nice being a prostitute and I am certain I never would have become one if I hadn't have been taken prisoner by that Arab.

'But it seems to me that there are only two types of people in this world — the givers and the takers. I tried the honest way, and it failed. Now I don't give a damn about anyone but myself ...'

18

With this Ring ...

'He only may chastise who loves.'
Rabidranath Tagore, 1913

Bad Harzburg, Germany, Autumn, 1994.

It is a typical German town, with buildings dating back to the fifteenth century and a stark greyness that is daunting for any visitor. Numerous tidy apartment blocks, never more than ten storeys high, provide a bleak backdrop, while the townsfolk rarely smile and tend to get on with the job at hand.

Provincial German towns frequently have that cold atmosphere in the daytime and seem only to come alive when darkness has fallen and the nightlife takes over to become the lifeblood of virtually every male under the age of 60.

There is a commonly held belief about this stark contrast: the Germans work very hard to earn a living, which means they tend to play even harder.

A night on the town in Bad Harzburg was usually a three-stage affair for the typical, lively male resident out with his friends. Naturally, food would come first and that usually meant a vast three- or four-course meal in one of the town's many restaurants. Sauerkraut and sausages, lashings of roast pork. All washed down with huge litre mugs of beer. Then your typical group would wander off to one of the livelier bars in Bad Harzburg where they would regale each other with blustery tales, covering a range of topics from soccer to politics. By about 9.30pm everyone would be well and truly on the way to drink-induced euphoria. This was when the insatiable appetite for sex usually took over.

Men would flock to the brothels on the edge of Bad Harzburg. All the townsfolk knew they were there, but they did not want to hear about or ever publicly acknowledge their existence.

Names like 'The Pink Pussycat' and 'The LA Club' were popular. The Germans have always felt more reassured by brothels with American-sounding names. They like those glamorous titles because that makes them feel they are the real thing.

But the set-up in each of those houses of ill-repute was basically the same: the customers paid a nominal entrance fee; then they would stroll up to the bar and order a drink. Suddenly, at least six girls, in skimpy basques, stockings and stilettos would appear, as if by magic, and start flirting outrageously.

Men on their first visit nearly always actually believed the girls were interested in their good looks and magnetic personalities. The fact that the girls were virtually naked and might possibly be more concerned with how much cash they could earn from such an assignation seemed not to strike them.

Dietmar Abke and Bernd Czerwinsky were two of the more experienced members of the brothel scene in Bad Harzburg in the autumn of 1994. Both of them were well known in some of the more brutal, sado-masochistic brothels, where customers demanded some appallingly perverted practices.

The fact that Abke, aged 31, had been married to a gorgeous blonde girl called Marita for more than a year did absolutely nothing to curtail his sexual demands as far as the dominatrixes of Bad Harzburg were concerned. Meanwhile, bachelor Czerwinsky's sick and twisted sexual habits had become so excessive that many of the prostitutes he encountered refused to have sex with him.

Czerwinksy was particularly fond of bullwhipping girls until they bled. He was also renowned for being an extremely penny-pinching guy who would always try to beat the girls down on price while expecting to beat them up in reality. Czerwinsky's sexual depravity had become so unpleasant by the middle of 1994 that he was actually finding it virtually impossible to hire a prostitute prepared to put up with his demands.

Meanwhile his weaker, married friend Dietmar Abke was starting to get clumsy with the perpetual lies he told his wife about where he went until the early hours most Friday and Saturday nights.

Marita Abke was a real head-turner and she was

starting to grow rather frustrated at her husband's complete refusal to include her in any of his social activities. Even worse, he would arrive home so drunk in the early hours of the morning that he was incapable of making love to her.

Inevitably, Marita started to get very irritated with her new husband. She began to interrogate him about his habits. This annoyed Abke a great deal because he felt it was none of her business. 'I pay the rent and I make sure you have a good life. What is your problem, woman?' he screamed at her drunkenly, after arriving home from some brothel or other early one morning.

'I know you have another woman, Dietmar. It's so obvious. Why don't you admit it?' Marita yelled back furiously. Within seconds, Abke was snoring his head off and poor Marita was left alone to fume about the state of her marriage.

Not surprisingly, the rows between the couple grew more and more heated as the months progressed. On his regular trips to the brothels, Abke found himself growing increasingly violent towards the prostitutes he slept with. It was almost as if he was taking out his anger and frustration on them rather than on his wife.

Meanwhile, his friend Bernd Czerwinsky was becoming equally frustrated by the fact that he was having more and more difficulty finding a prostitute prepared to put up with the horrendous beatings he wanted to inflict on them. One night the two men were drowning their sorrows before yet another sortie to a brothel when Abke surprised his friend by starting openly to criticise his wife. 'I'm fed up of her nagging. She just won't leave me alone. She thinks I've got a girlfriend. It's getting ridiculous,' he complained to Czerwinsky.

In Abke's mind, sleeping with prostitutes did not count as adultery. He simply thought of them as providing a service for a guy who knew he could not get his sexual kicks at home. Czerwinsky was actually rather jealous of his friend, because he seemed to have the best of both worlds. He had a beautiful wife at home and a number of prostitutes on tap. Czerwinsky was particularly envious because he had always thought that Marita was incredibly attractive.

'You don't know how lucky you are,' said Czerwinsky. 'If I had a wife like Marita ...'

'You'd beat the shit out of her,' laughed Abke, 'I know what turns you on.'

Czerwinsky hit back coolly. 'You're dead right. I would.'

A brief silence followed. Then Czerwinsky took a deep breath before continuing, 'If you're so pissed off with her, I'll take her off your hands.'

'What?' exclaimed an astonished Abke.

'I mean it. I think she's an incredibly sexy girl. I've always fancied her.'

'No way.'

'It's just a thought. Nothing more.'

Abke quickly changed the subject, but he knew that his friend meant every word of what he had said.

A few beers later, the conversation returned to Marita. 'Did you mean it?' asked Abke.

'Mean what?'

'That you'd take Marita off my hands.'

'Of course I did. I'd pay you a lot of money to have

my way with her.'

'You're kidding.'

'You want a bet?'

'How much?'

'Fifty thousand marks [£22,700].'

Dietmar Abke paused for a second as he absorbed the significance of their conversation. His best friend had just offered him fifty thousand marks to have sex with his wife. It seemed like the perfect answer. He would be rid of her nagging ways and he would make some much-needed extra cash.

Just then, Czerwinsky butted in. 'But you'd have to let me do what I want to her. I might keep her for days. You can have her back whenever I don't need her.'

Abke knew perfectly well what his friend would do to his wife, yet he found the scheme very appealing — except for one big problem.

'She'd never agree.'

'She would if you had some hold over her. Like threatening to kill her parents if she didn't cooperate.' Czerwinsky was capable of carrying out such a threat and that made it all the more terrifying. By the end of that evening this dreadful, perverted deal had been struck and Marita Abke's fate sealed.

The following night, Abke explained to his wife what he had done. Not surprisingly, she went wild with anger. That is a pity, thought Abke, it means I will have to tie her up. He then bundled her into the back of his car and drove her to Czerwinsky's apartment on the other side of town.

Once inside the flat, he pushed his terrified wife on to the bed and then demanded his fifty thousand marks. Czerwinsky paid up immediately and told his friend to leave.

'I'll call you when I've finished with her,' he said, looking hungrily at Marita,

Abke did not feel a twinge of guilt and left the apartment immediately. That will teach her a lesson she will never forget, he thought to himself. Less than an hour later, Marita Abke was being locked in wooden stocks in a torture room that Czerwisnky had created to try to feed his evil habits.

When she screamed, he shoved a leather hood over her head and then laughed before he submitted her to the first of many painful beatings.

For the following two days, Marita was abused in such a vicious fashion that it is not possible to repeat the details here. But suffice to say, Czerwinsky's perverted habits knew no boundaries. At one stage he even hired a prostitute to beat Marita while he watched. He also forced her to drink alcohol and take drugs.

By the time she was returned to her husband, Marita was a broken wreck. It took her more than a week to recover physically from her ordeal and return to her job as a secretary. She thought about telling her colleagues what had happened, but kept thinking back to her husband's threat to kill her parents if she dared tell anyone. The mental scars would haunt her for ever.

Back at home, she shook with fear each time the telephone rang in case it was Czerwinsky. Strangely, her husband Dietmar had actually been nicer to her since he had struck that dreadful deal with his friend. Marita suspected it was because he was rather turned on by the thought of his wife getting beaten black and blue by another man.

A few days later, Czerwinsky called up and demanded that Marita be made available for another perverted sex session. This time, Marita pleaded with her husband not to make her go.

'I can't stand it. It's so horrible. Please, I'll do anything if you tell him I can't do it. Please.'

But Abke would not budge. 'I made a deal with Bernd and I don't see why I should go back on it.'

Marita then flung herself at her husband's feet.

'You can't do this to me. You can't.'

'I can,' said Abke, as he felt inside his pocket for something. 'Now you'd better do as I say.'

But Marita was shaking her head furiously.

'No. No. No.'

Abke flicked on his cigarette lighter and held it under his wife's wrist. She screamed but he held her wrist firmly in one hand while burning it with the other.

'Yes, you will.'

Those dreadful sex sessions with the twisted sadist Czerwinsky went on for months, and eventually Marita fell into a zombie-like state every time her husband forced her to go to his friend's torture chamber apartment.

Her wrists were scarred from where she had been forced to sit in the wooden stocks and her body was covered in bruises and cuts from the beatings he had inflicted on her. She had been beaten into submission. She no longer fought against her husband, but he still insisted on trussing her up like a turkey before taking her round to Czerwinsky's cold, damp apartment.

At home, there was virtually no communication

between Marita and her husband. He had started prowling the red-light districts of the town virtually every night and Marita was so exhausted by stress and fear that she would usually fall asleep by 10pm each evening.

This time, it was Dietmar Abke who had the look of sheer terror on his face. Marita smiled with satisfaction. A few minutes earlier, she had smashed him over the head with a hammer as he walked into their home. Now he was the one bound by rope to a chair that stood in the middle of the living room.

She walked around and around her husband and smacked him across the face every few seconds. 'I haven't decided what I'm going to do with you, but it will hurt more than anything I have had to put up with,' Marita screamed at her husband.

Abke looked pale and pathetic. Marita picked up a rolling pin and smashed it against the side of his face. She could hear his teeth cracking. Her husband sobbed and pleaded for mercy. 'Bastard. You're going to pay for what you've done to me,' muttered Marita.

Just then she awoke from her dream. To anyone else it would have been a nightmare, but to Marita it was an inspiration. She had enjoyed that dream so much that she knew she had to get a grip on herself and do something to stop her husband and his evil friend from continuing to use her as a sex slave. She lay in bed and started to formulate a plan. Each time she thought of a punishment for her husband it was more extreme. By the time she had finalised her scheme, she had decided that Dietmar was going to pay the ultimate price.

The following evening, Marita was waiting for her husband to come home from work so she could take her revenge. When he finally appeared, she attacked him so swiftly with a carving knife that he was killed from a dozen stab wounds before he even knew what had happened.

Then Marita decided to disembowel her husband and rid herself of every piece of him for ever. She started cutting his flesh into tiny pieces but found herself overwhelmed with guilt about what she had just done. A few days later, she confessed to police that she had murdered her husband. But when detectives heard about her horrific life at the hands of Abke and Czerwinsky, they promised her they would do everything in their power to help her.

In October, 1995, at a court in Braunschweig, Marita admitted to killing her husband, but the judge set her free after hearing about her hellish life at the hands of those two sadistic monsters.

19

Sold by her Family

'Take this sorrow to thy heart, and make it a part of thee, and it shall nourish thee till thou art strong again.'

Hyperion, Longfellow, 1839

Freetown, Sierra Leone, Summer, 1993.

It is a sprawling city skirted by some of the worst shanty towns in the world. Yet, ironically, Sierra Leone was established as a British naval base in 1807 to help prevent the prolific trade in human slaves shipped from West Africa to the four corners of the globe.

By all accounts, the British had a tough time curtailing the flow of human cargo. Many observers complained that the local people were simply too pleasant and amenable — making them perfect fodder for cold-hearted slave masters seeking out suitable humans to trade for cash. Now, almost two hundred years later, that illicit trade still flourishes ...

Little nine-year-old Hawa lived with her mother and six brothers and sisters in Wilkinson Road, Freetown, in a simple, wooden shanty with a corrugated iron roof held up by a few beams. As with most African families, the cooking was always done outside on a camp-fire. Water was obtained from a nearby well and toilet facilities consisted of a ditch at the back of the house.

Hawa's mother, Yaya, had always had to struggle to bring up her children — two other sons had died in infancy. Her husband had been killed in a road accident just before Hawa's seventh birthday. Yaya barely scraped a living by growing vegetables on a small plot behind the house. She also obtained rice for the family from her brother in exchange for her help at harvest time on his land, eighty miles east of Freetown. But that was a risky venture as it involved leaving the children in the care of Hawa.

So when Lebanese trader Abdullah befriended the family, they were most grateful. Every now and then, he would appear at the shack with small gifts of milk and sometimes even meat for Yaya and her brood. They never once questioned his motives. That simply was not the way their minds worked.

Abdullah was a well-known figure in the bustling commercial centre of Freetown, where he owned numerous clothes and jewellery stores — as did thousands of other Lebanese traders who had settled in Sierra Leone following the outbreak of war in their home country.

But one day, the 52-year-old Arab appeared at the entrance to the shack bearing more gifts for Yaya and her children with a blatant, ulterior motive. 'It is time you let me give Hawa a good home away from all this,' he explained patiently to Yaya. Then he produced a contract. It read:

An Agreement made the 27th day of September 1980 betwwen Abdullah ——— of Freetown, Sierra Leone (hereafter called the employer) and Da Mende ——— of Freetown, Sierra Leone.

Whereas Hawa ——— is in the employment of Abdullah ——— as housemaid and in the course of her employment is requested to travel to the Lebanon.

Abdullah had signed the contract himself. Hawa's uncle had already been approached by the Arab and left his thumbprint because he could not write, and Hawa herself would later manage an almost illegible scrawl as her signature. Like any good mother, Yaya wanted only what was best for her daughter. She looked around at the mud-encrusted shack and knew there had to be a better life for Hawa elsewhere, even if it meant seperating her from her loved ones.

According to the World Health Organization, life expectancy in Sierra Leone has remained the lowest of any country in the world — an average of 41 years compared with well over 70 years in Britain and the United States. In these conditions, where life is so cheap, one less mouth to feed could mean the survival of the rest of the family.

Abdullah then went on to explain to Yaya that he 'represented' some other Lebanese traders who had returned to Beirut and wanted Hawa to work for them. The little girl sat just outside the entrance to the shack and listened intently to every word he was saying. She was confused. She had heard of many young girls who had gone to work for rich foreigners and never returned to their families. It had always been presumed that they had gone to live a better life away from the poverty and deprivation of the slums. This was an opportunity to escape the misery, but it also might mean never seeing her family again.

Hawa started quietly sobbing as she contemplated a future without her family. Her mother had warned her that this day might come and had tried to explain to Hawa that there simply was not enough food for the entire family. This was, in the words of her mother, a golden opportunity.

'Hawa, come here and talk to the gentleman,' said Yaya, shaking the young girl out of her thoughts and back to reality.

Hawa got up and walked into the shack. Abdullah turned towards her, an oily smile spreading across his face. 'You are going to nice people. They will look after you well and send you to school.'

He hesitated at that moment, then looked across at Yaya, who had an expectant expression on her face.

'They will pay you every month and I will pass the money on to your mother.'

Yaya looked quietly satisfied. She had been desperately looking for a means to increase her minimal income and her nine-year-old daughter was about to provide it.

Hawa put her only belongings in a plastic shopping bag and then ran to Abdullah's Mercedes waiting in the muddy, washed-out track that ran along the front of the shack. A few moments later, as the car pulled away, she wondered if she would ever see her family again ...

Some hours later, Hawa was going down the runway in one of those big white birds that flew low over her shanty town every day. There was nothing she could do to prevent herself from being sent to Beirut. She was just nine years old. She had to trust Abdullah and hope that everything would turn out OK.

When the plane touched down in Beirut, a driver was waiting to whisk her off to an apartment block in Verdun Street, in the Muslim west side of the city. The house belonged to local police chief Ben Luyinda and his wife, Aliya. They were Hawa's master and mistress. Hawa was never formally introduced to them, but she was completely overawed by the vast apartment the moment she stepped into it.

It was beautiful! Hawa dropped her belongings and ran over to the windows to look at the street below. She had never experienced such a view before. She turned back to look around the room. Woven rugs lay scattered across the pale, polished wooden floor, and the furniture was even arranged so that no one need sit with their back to the scenery. Natural canvas and heavy Muslim artifacts dominated the decor and a desk stood in the corner opposite the windows. Natural light poured in as Hawa looked in wonder at the antique painted pottery on the shelves of a glass-fronted cabinet and the framed photos on one wall, showing her master and mistress and their children.

It was only as Hawa was being told by the other servants never to use the same cutlery as the family who now owned her, that she learned the name of her employers. She was given her own plate, fork, knife and cup. She looked bewildered. Less than a day earlier, she had been living with her mother and brothers and sisters in a mud hut. Just thinking about them made her burst into tears. She was a child in a strange country without a friend or relative.

'Stop crying, girl!' screeched a voice from the front door. There was not a hint of sympathy in Aliya Luyinda's voice when she saw little Hawa sobbing. 'You cannot go home. You must stay here and work for us. We own you.'

If Hawa had been a little older she might have appreciated the full meaning of those words. But as it was, she had only just begun a sentence as a slave that would go on for many, many years.

'There are no schools for black people in Beirut. You stay here. You do not go out. Do you understand?'

Hawa nodded her head as Aliya yelled at her yet again, just a few days after her arrival in Beirut. She had dared to ask about Abdullah's promise of education. Now she realised there was no point in pursuing the subject. The only things she was going to be taught involved housework, preparing food and waiting at table. Soon Hawa was cooking for as many as thirty people whenever the Luyindas held dinner parties. She worked every day from 6.00am to midnight, sometimes even later if the family felt like staying up.

Hawa was forbidden to eat until everything in the house had been cleared up. She frequently fell asleep in her food — often only hard crusts of bread and regurgitated meat, spat out on to the plate by one of the Luyindas' guests.

Humiliation was a popular pastime for Aliya and her husband. When little Hawa did not clear the plates fast enough or cook the food on time, they would grab her by the hair and tell her, 'Faster! Slave! Faster! What have you been doing?'

Sometimes, when she was serving her master and mistress, Hawa would be made to crawl on all fours across the floor before getting up and clearing the table. Aliya told the child that neither she nor her husband wanted to look at her face. Later, Hawa concluded that whenever they saw her eyes, they felt guilty about their abuse of her.

One day, Hawa spilt some soup on the marble floor of the dining room. Ben Luyinda exploded as his wife looked on contentedly.

'Dog! Clear it up! Now!'

Hawa was frozen to the spot with fear. But her lack of movement was interpreted as defiance by the police chief. He grabbed her by the wrist and pulled her over his lap. Then she felt the leather sole of his shoe beating her.

At the other end of the table Aliya watched with cold satisfaction. As Ben continued beating the child, she felt his other hand sliding between her legs. She struggled to free herself, but he just beat her harder and his fingers probed deeper.

'Maybe we should just kill her?' Aliya said from her vantage point.

'No. That would be too good for her.

At that moment, Ben removed the belt from his trousers and pushed Hawa forward over the dining room table before beating her at least a dozen more times.

That night, Hawa cried herself to sleep. She was so confused. Anything, even life back in the slums, had to be better than this.

Hawa was trapped in a little steel box, the burning walls tight against her flesh on all sides. The air was musty and smelled bitter, like chemicals spilling over copper. She could not see anything in the darkness, and no one could get to her, no one could let her out before the sun burnt through the steel and melted it against her body in running rivulets, scorching her, going through her, until she screamed and screamed and ran out of air and could not breathe ...

Flames touched her, and she jerked awake. Instantly, the pain of her nightmare became her real-life suffering. She moaned, and something searing touched her again. This time, Hawa realised that it was not fire at all, but the pain of her bruises and bumps where Ben had hit her.

Hawa was lying on her side, and as she drew in a harsh breath, she inhaled a mouthful of dust. It did not make her dry mouth and throat any better. As she began to cough up blood, she opened her eyes. Her right eye. Her left eye, still pressed against the surface she was lying on, was swollen. It opened only a slit, and that scared her more than anything else.

She could focus on something long and brown, with a brush at the end of it — the broom. She was on the floor of the broom closet, next to the hallway. They had not even let her sleep in the tiny room she called a bedroom. Just dumped her in an filthy closet, to lie in the dust and dirt. Hawa started to cry again and found that even that hurt. From the crown of her head to the soles of her feet, she was nothing but a mass of pain.

I want to go home, she thought, clenching her hands into fists. 'I don't care anymore, I just want to go home, where I can be with my own family and never have to take this from someone who could just do it without any reason!' She sobbed heavily, and each movement of her body seemed to discover another bruised inch of aching flesh. Somehow her exhaustion and despair overcame her pain, and she fell into a fitful sleep, drifting back and forth between vivid nightmares and agonising consciousness.

Ben and his wife soon stepped up the number of beatings they gave Hawa. As the only full-time servant in the Luyindas' four-bedroom apartment, there were many things to do every day. She had to struggle out on to the verandah with a huge carpet and beat every speck of dust out of it. Then she had to water every one of the hundreds of plants scattered all around the apartment. Aliya had warned Hawa that if any of them died, then she would be beaten severely. Hawa was even expected to wash every single leaf.

Then there were the mirrors, windows and floors that had to be polished to perfection. Hawa found herself praying to God every night that she would not get sick because the Luyindas would never allow her to see a doctor, let alone take time off if she felt unwell.

After more than a year as a slave to the Luyindas,

Hawa felt all emotion beginning to drain from her. During those first twelve months she had cried so much that it was difficult to shed any more tears. She had learnt how to repress her true emotions for fear that the Luyindas might see them and use it as an excuse to beat her.

The worst attack of all had occurred when Ben had arrived home drunk after a police function. His wife was away visiting relatives and he was so inebriated that he was incapable of opening the front door with his key. When Hawa answered it, his face lit up with lust.

'Why did you take so long, dog?'

Hawa did not answer. She knew that to reply would seem insolent. She did not want to make things any worse for herself.

As she closed the door behind the sweating, overweight Ben, she smelt the stench of alcohol on his breath. She turned to walk towards her tiny bedroom, when he caught her wrist and swung her around, crushing her slight body against his.

'Talk dog. Say something!'

'Yes, master,' was all poor little Hawa could reply. She was shaking with fear, horribly aware of what might be about to follow.

Suddenly, Ben grabbed a clump of her hair in his other hand and began dragging the girl along the hallway floor. Hawa did not utter another sound that night. She just stared at the ceiling once they got to Ben's bedroom and tried to think of the better life that she was sure existed somewhere outside this prison.

She tried hard to divert her thoughts, but every word that animal said, the images they evoked, the incredible humiliation of it all was too overwhelming.

This was truly hell on earth.

Two days passed in a blur of pain, humiliation and constant agony. Ben ran Hawa ragged, making her rise before dawn so that she could begin cleaning the apartment, and then keeping her up late at night, punishing her. He never once stopped to ask about her feelings. When there were no real chores to be done, Ben became the master of 'make-work', and Hawa knew that when the mistress got back, she would be coming home to an apartment that had been scrubbed and polished from floor to ceiling and then back again. Every shoe or boot in the closets, every toy in the children's room, every piece of artwork, every dish, glass and pot, every inch of wooden floor and furniture and every piece of metal in the apartment had been individually and perfectly cleaned, polished and buffed.

It did not take long for the bruises to start showing through the pink and red of Hawa's beaten flesh. There was no escape from the near-constant pain of her body. Her movements from walking to sleeping, were all accompanied by sharp stabbing pain and throbbing aches — all reminders of the torture inflicted on her over the previous days.

On the second night, Ben chained her to the end of his bed like a rabid dog and at regular intervals unlocked the padlock and forced her to perform. For the first time in her miserable life, Hawa actually prayed to be locked up because at least that meant he would leave her alone.

On the last morning before the mistress arrived home, Hawa was unchained and told to get to work. She soon became aware of Ben following her from room to room, his eyes boring into her.

'Do not tell anyone about this,' he cautioned her. 'Do not breathe a word about what has happened.'

He looked her in the eye one last time before he left her to continue with her chores. 'If you embarrass me,' he whispered, trailing one finger down between her breasts, 'I'll kill you. Do you understand?'

'Yes sir,' Hawa whispered back. For a moment, her body started to shake uncontrollably, but she clenched her teeth, determined not to reveal the full extent of her fear.

Hawa was never allowed out of the Beirut apartment, except to walk across the street to the bakery for some bread. But her occasional tastes of freedom proved almost as unpleasant as her life behind the closed doors of the Luyinda household.

As she crossed the street to the bakery, local children and adults would hurl racist insults in her direction. They liked to call her 'chocolate' and shouted Arabic words meaning banana and water melon.

The second time she went to the bakery, a rock hit her on the head. She turned to look where it had come from and saw a man in his twenties sneering at her.

'Nigger girl. Go home!'

If only I could, thought Hawa. I would give anything to get out of this devil's playground and return to the shanty town.

Just then, three more rocks showered down on her. She knew she could not return to the apartment empty-handed, because the Luyindas would beat her for failing in her duties. Hawa heard gunfire and explosions in the distance as the war in Beirut raged on. But her only battle at that time was to survive.

As the months turned into years, Hawa started to lose track of time. She was banned from seeing anything that might actually tell her what date or even what year it was. After a couple of years, she stopped celebrating her birthday because she did not know when it was and nobody seemed to care.

She no longer even knew her own age. She was never taught to read or write. She was living a highly restricted life, in a city she had only briefly glimpsed en route from the airport all those years before.

Hawa did manage to form a tentative friendship with Vera, another girl from Sierra Leone, who worked as a slave for a Lebanese family in the same apartment block. But both girls were extremely careful not to allow their respective families to find out, because they knew they would be punished.

Unable to write, Hawa relied on Vera to write letters to her family back in Freetown. But she never received any replies, apart from two letters which were sent to Vera. Hawa started to suspect that whenever she left letters for the postman, the Luyindas would simply destroy them when she was not looking.

Then in 1985, at the age of fifteen, Hawa suddenly found herself being bundled off to Beirut airport to be flown back to Freetown. The teenager was confused. The Luyindas had always told her that she belonged to them and would never be able to go home. Now, for no apparent reason, she was about to have her dream realised. Or was she?

Aliya Luyinda told Hawa that she was being taken back to Sierra Leone to renew her passport. Since the document had been confiscated the moment she arrived in Beirut, Hawa had no idea she even had one in the first place.

But Hawa's face dropped when she was met at Freetown airport by Abdullah, the man who had been responsible for all the misery she had endured over the previous years. He took her arm and guided her to his Mercedes. Hawa, more assertive than before, tried to fathom out from the Arab what was happening. She wanted to know if she could stay in Freetown. She certainly never wanted to go back to that apartment in Beirut ever again.

'I want the money that you promised to pay my family. I know you have never given it to them,' she told him.

Abdullah raised his hands in surrender.

'Of course. I made a contract and I have no intention of breaking that agreement.'

Hawa was mildly surprised. She had expected him to try to avoid paying any of the money owed to her and her family. He seemed to be acting in an honourable manner.

Abdullah pulled out his wallet and counted out $65.

'There you are.'

Hawa looked at the money in disgust.

'What is this? You owe my family much more than that. I have been away for years.'

The problem was that Hawa did not actually know how long she had been away. She thought it was a couple of years but she could not be sure.

'I'll pay your mother the rest of the money when you go back to Beirut ...'

Hawa was stunned at what she was hearing. She had no intention of returning to that city.

'But ... I am home now.'

Abdullah completely ignored Hawa and continued, 'Your mother needs this money very badly. I am offering to pay her the entire amount on condition you go back to Beirut. You have no choice.'

'But my family is here.'

'Your family don't need you here but they do need your money.'

Hawa sunk into the seat in the back of Abdullah's Mercedes. She was trapped. Nowhere to turn. She could not quite believe that she was back in her home town but unable to stay. She pleaded with Abdullah to let her remain a few days with her mother.

'OK. But you must go back to Beirut when I say.' Hawa agreed, although she secretly hoped that she could change the situation. She just needed a bit of time. But one problem Hawa did not allow for was her mother.

Yaya made it clear from the moment her daughter arrived back at that old familiar shack on the outskirts of the city that she did not want Hawa around. Yaya saw the shapely teenager as a threat to the peace and tranquillity of her home. Local men kept calling round at the hut after hearing about how Hawa had blossomed into an attractive young woman. Yaya felt threatened. She was used to being the only adult female in the household. In any case, she wanted Hawa to go back to Beirut to earn the remainder of the money Abdullah had promised.

One night, Hawa sat down with her mother after the other children had gone to bed and tried to explain how awful her life in Beirut had been. But Yaya closed her ears to it. She believed that Hawa was lying. How could life be that bad in such a civilised country?

Within hours of Hawa getting her new passport, Abdullah was taking her back to the airport to get on the plane. If anything, she felt even more demoralised than the last time she had made the trip, because now not even her mother seemed prepared to offer her love.

When Hawa arrived back in Beirut, she found that the civil war had intensified and the large apartment block where the Luyindas lived was regularly caught in the crossfire. Many Arab families left the city during this period, but Ben Luyinda — now a general in the Muslim forces — insisted his family remain.

As the bombs and sniper fire rained down on them, the Luyindas decided that life might be safer if they moved to the shelters built in the basement of the block. They left Hawa to live in the apartment on her own.

'We don't want the black slave too close to us,' she overheard Aliya telling her husband. Hawa also believed that Aliya did not want her to have any opportunity to be alone with her husband. Just before they evacuated, Aliya had pulled Hawa aside and warned her to keep away from Ben 'unless I am in the room'.

So, with bombs and snipers constantly pounding the building, Hawa was left alone while the Luyindas lived in comparative safety downstairs in the basement. Frequently, she found herself cowering in the passageway in the middle of the apartment while bullets whistled through the windows, some of them at such high velocity that they pierced the plaster walls.

One time, she crawled on her hands and knees to

the front door as explosions ripped all around her. Gasping for breath, she pulled open the door only to be confronted by a hooded gunman spraying his machine-gun at the ceiling of the hallway.

'Get back! Get back!' he screamed at her. She slammed the door shut and sat huddled in a corner praying that he would not burst into the apartment. To this day, she does not know why he did not kill her.

But the worst aspect of being in that flat during the attacks was the loneliness. It was not as if she enjoyed the company of the Luyindas, but she did feel there was some safety in numbers. Sometimes Hawa — still only fifteen years old — was so frightened that she could not stop shaking. On at least one occasion she found herself so paralysed with fear that she urinated on the spot where she crouched from the warring factions blasting away just outside the building. When the bombing subsided that day, she was just as frightened that the Luyindas would return to the apartment and discover what she had done.

After months of enduring the relentless bombardment, Hawa started to believe that perhaps she would be better off dead. Once, as blasts shook the very foundations of the apartment block, Hawa walked on to the balcony of the building and started talking to herself. 'Let them kill me! My life is nothing. I would be better off dead.'

As Hawa stood there, she saw many people lying dead in the street below. She felt a wave of envy for them. At least their battle was over. She watched as a man was stabbed to death by another, following ferocious hand-to-hand combat. Then Hawa leaned over the balcony to see a man three storeys below her. He had something in his hand — it might have been a grenade or maybe a cluster bomb. Just then, another man appeared with a rifle and moved swiftly across the street. At that moment the man on the balcony dropped the bomb directly on to the man's head. It exploded on impact, decapitating the man.

In the middle of all this carnage, Hawa's mistress Aliya would telephone her from the family's basement hideaway demanding that she bring them food and drink. 'And make it quick. We are very hungry and thirsty,' Aliya told her young slave girl, completely disregarding the threat of bombs and bullets.

Hawa did not dare point out the obvious: that she would be risking her life by leaving the apartment at that particular moment. Instead, she replaced the receiver and started to prepare the food. A little later, she struggled along the halfway of the apartment with the food on a tray before scrambling down the many flights of steps to the basement.

Aliya was not exactly grateful. 'Next time make more. We get very hungry down here.' As Hawa turned to leave, Aliya remembered something else. 'And don't forget to clean the flat of all the broken glass before we come back.'

During a break in fighting a few months later, Aliya called Hawa into the living room. Her beautiful blonde 23-year-old daughter, Zeina, was there. Hawa had long since despised this girl, with her designer-label clothes and sneering expression. When she was a teenager, Zeina had been ruthless and cruel to Hawa, taunting her about her race and even the size of her breasts. 'I have a new job for you,' said Aliya. 'From now on you are Zeina's slave.'

Hawa said nothing. But then Zeina spoke. 'Thank you, Mommy. Thank you so much. She is the best wedding present I could ever hope for.'

It was then that Hawa realised she had been given to Zeina as a gift for her forthcoming wedding to Aku Koto. Within weeks, Hawa was on her way to a new country with her young, arrogant mistress. When the young girl had heard it was London, the capital city of England, she felt that perhaps her nightmare might be slowly coming to an end. Surely there was no way that Zeina could keep her as a slave in such a civilised society? Slavery was outlawed in places like London. Or so Hawa thought.

But the drudgery worsened in London. The family lived in a mansion just a stone's throw from Regent's Park. Hawa found herself working as housemaid, cook, butler and nanny to Zeina's baby. She started work before five every morning and did not stop before midnight. It was a relentless, seven-days-a-week existence and she never received a penny in wages.

By the end of 1986, Hawa was in her seventh year of slavery. She still could not read or write. She was terrified to leave of the house because Zeina had told her there were rapists and murderers on every street corner. The windows to the house were barred and a sophisticated alarm system was tripped the moment anyone tried to enter or leave the premises. At night, private security guards patrolled the grounds at two-hour intervals. It was a fortress in the middle of a country that Hawa had thought was a bastion of freedom.

Whenever Zeina left the house, she went to enormous lengths to lock Hawa in. Her initial promise of providing Hawa with some form of education was rapidly forgotten. The Kotos had a BMW, a Mercedes and a Bentley in the driveway, but they never once offered to pay for anything for Hawa, let alone hand over the salary that had been promised that day in Freetown when Abdullah had made his offer to Hawa's family.

With absolutely nothing to lose, Hawa began to try to persuade the hard-nosed Zeina to let her benefit from some form of education in London. Finally, after months of asking, Zeina arranged for Hawa to go to English classes for just one hour a week. She was to be accompanied by the family's chauffeur, who would take her directly home once the class had finished.

Hawa found it so strange being out in the big, wide world. She felt extremely nervous and wary of talking to anyone, especially after the ominous warning given to her by Zeina just after they arrived in London. In the classroom, Hawa had great difficulty concentrating because she was so scared of being out on her own. It must be remembered that she had not been given this much freedom since those far-off days in the slums of Freetown.

'What is the matter, Hawa?' asked her teacher one day.

The teenager was too frightened to respond.

'Nothing, Sir,' was all she could say.

Hawa did consider telling her teacher the truth about her awful life of slavery. But then she remembered what Zeina had told her just before she started school. 'Don't even think about telling anyone about your life here because if you lose this job, the police will throw you out of the country. You will get into a lot of trouble. Maybe you will even be killed.'

Back in the classroom, Hawa's teacher repeated the question. 'Are you sure there is nothing wrong?'

Hawa shivered with fear and trepidation. She dared not say anything. That afternoon, Hawa's teacher rang Zeina to ask her why Hawa had been acting so strangely. It was a caring thought on the part of the teacher, but unfortunately it sparked off a tirade of further abuse against the young girl.

After just four lessons, Zeina forbade Hawa to go to school any more. 'You cannot be trusted. You will stay here all the time,' was her explanation to Hawa.

The only aspect of Hawa's life that was any more bearable in London was that at least she did not have to contend with the lecherous Ben Luyinda forcing her to have sex.

Hawa befriended a West Indian woman called Mary, who came in to help with the cleaning of the large house and struck up conversations with Hawa despite Zeina's obvious disapproval. Zeina deliberately forced her two servants to work at opposite ends of the house so that it would be virtually impossible for them to communicate. But Mary had recognised in Hawa a needy soul from the moment they had met and she was determined to get to know the young woman.

Whenever Zeina went to the gym for a work-out or disappeared to the beautician or hairdresser, Mary would seek out Hawa and talk to her. Sometimes they would chat together for hours and Mary gradually pieced together the details of Hawa's sad and tragic life as a slave girl.

Mary was shocked when she discovered that not only did Hawa's working day start earlier and end much later than hers, but she had never once been paid. And when Hawa told her that she was not allowed out of the house, not even as far as the wrought-iron gates at the end of the driveway, Mary became even more determined to help the young girl.

She invited Hawa to stay at her home for Christmas that year because she could not stand the thought of that poor girl remaining all alone in the house on such a festive occasion. But Zeina and her husband soon put a stop to such plans. 'You will stay here. You will never leave the house,' the young wife told her slave. 'Remember what I told you. If you disobey us, you will be thrown out of the country.'

Hawa did not argue with her mistress.

Zeina continued, 'I may do as I like to you, and need not seek your consent. I do not owe you any explanation. You are just a person who belongs to me, and nothing more, do you understand?'

That evening, Zeina beat Hawa black and blue with a horsewhip when she failed to close the door behind her after she had served her mistress her supper in the living room. Hawa remained silent as Mary washed her down with a towel and tried to soothe her bruised skin. She offered Hawa a bottle of fresh water which she took eagerly. The water tasted sweet and wonderful and, for a moment, almost seemed to banish the throbbing pains that wracked her poor body.

Mary laughed dryly as she accepted the young girl's apologies about why she had to work that

Christmas and could not visit her home. Despite the pain of that thrashing, Hawa was still worrying about upsetting her only friend. It was a touching gesture.

As Mary helped Hawa get dressed, she was seething at the treatment being meted out to her young friend. She was further infuriated when she discovered that many of the letters she had written for Hawa to her family were thrown away by Zeina before they could be posted.

Worse still, only a handful of letters from Hawa's family in West Africa were given to Hawa, which could only mean one thing — Zeina was throwing these away as well.

Mary advised Hawa to try to collect the post before Zeina every morning because she would probably never hand over the letters from Hawa's family. It had become clear to Mary that Hawa was being treated appallingly. She begged her young friend to consider running away but those threats from Zeina were constantly ringing in Hawa's ears. She was also terrified of what life would be like in the world outside.

'Up until then I did not realise how unhappy I was,' she recalls. 'Until now. Until I thought that there was a life on the outside. Oh, God, how did I get into this? How did I allow myself to be used and abused?'

When Mary decided to leave Zeina's employment to take on another, better-paid job, Hawa was very upset because Mary had become her only real contact with the world beyond those four walls.

But Mary had already decided that, with nothing to lose, she was going to help Hawa escape. She began to formulate a clever scheme that she believed was completely airtight. It involved persuading Zeina to take on Mary's sister, Denise, as a part-time cleaner while she was looking for a new employee.

Denise was more than happy to play a role in the scheme once she had been told of Hawa's plight. The two women sat Hawa down one day and explained in detail how they were going to bring her tortuous enslavement to an end.

A few days later the plan was put into operation. Denise made an excuse to Zeina as to why she had to stay late to finish polishing the silver in the dining-room. This meant Zeina would have to leave the house without locking the front door from the outside, as she always did whenever she left Hawa alone in the mansion. Within minutes of Zeina departing, Denise helped Hawa pack her few belongings and they left the house. Minutes later they caught a taxi to Mary's home five miles away, in north London. It had been a remarkably simple plan. But Hawa's problems were only just beginning.

It took two months of wrangling between police, social workers and the Kotos to get the Lebanese family to return Hawa's passport to her. When Hawa finally saw it, she learnt that her birthday was on 4 October. According to the passport, she was born in 1968 and so was nineteen years old when she escaped from the Kotos in 1987. She had actually believed she was only sixteen years old.

Her freedom brought with it many fresh problems. While enslaved in one of London's smartest areas, she had painstakingly learnt to write her name in joined-up letters, but could write little more. She had never been on a bus or the Underground, and had never even walked down a London street. Apart from Mary, she knew no one in London. She had no money, nowhere to live, and no legal right to reside in Britain. She did not want to return to Freetown because she knew her mother could not afford to keep her.

Eventually, after further months of legal wrangling, Hawa won the right to stay in Britain and she is now working and living with an English family in the London area. She remains very frightened of the outside world.

'I am just as scared now because I have no right place to live. No home, no country. If anything happens to me, no one knows where I am.'

Neither the Kotos, the Luyindas nor Abdullah, the man who originally sold Hawa into slavery, have ever been brought to justice for enslaving her for almost half her life.

Viola

'A slave must be intelligent, truthful, unique and loyal. Most of all she must have the time to prove herself to me.'

Mistress Mir, 1996

Two-Storey House, Tree-Lined Street, New Jersey, January 1996.

5.45am — the long, piercing tone of the alarm clock broke the silence. Viola snapped open her eyes and tried with difficulty to move in her narrow single bed, because skin-tight, black leather restraints were digging into her wrists and ankles. But she did not dare to utter a word in case her mistress got angry.

Yet another long and gruelling day as the ultimate slave was about to begin.

Viola had lain there, trapped, for eight hours

following an appalling beating at the hands of her employer. But unlike any other slave, Viola was not eaten up by fear of, or hatred for her mistress. Instead she felt a surge of excitement flow through her body as she thought about the brutal regime that she faced that and every day.

Two hours later, the door swung open and her mistress — a striking, glamorous African-American woman called Mir — strode into the room. Viola looked up fearfully and then shut her eyes tightly as her mistress slapped her across her face.

A few minutes later, with her first beating of the day over, Viola's wrists and ankles were unshackled. She stretched her body as she got out of bed and adjusted the leather collar round her neck, which represented more evidence of her enslavement. Viola enjoyed wearing the collar because it reminded her of her adoration for her mistress, Mir, the woman to whom she had become utterly devoted over the previous two years.

Incredibly, among the millions of women slaves today, there are estimated to be tens of thousands of voluntary slaves who have allowed themselves to become full-time devotees to masters and mistresses.

Viola is a classic example: she lives as a full-time slave to a beautiful woman in a quiet suburban New Jersey neighbourhood in the heart of middle America. Behind the closed doors of a beautifully decorated house worth many hundreds of thousands of dollars, Viola allows herself to be abused and beaten and humiliated for love of her mistress.

Viola even has Mir's name tattooed on her leg as a permanent reminder of her enslavement to her mistress.

She explains in all seriousness, 'I am her property. She can do what she wants to me. I have given my life to her.'

Viola's route to sexual enslavement is extraordinary, because she looks more like a plump, middle-aged housewife. But behind her calm demeanour and warm sense of humour lies a woman in turmoil, who has felt the need to offer herself completely and utterly to a mistress.

Up until her incarceration, she had suffered abuse at the hands of uncaring, disloyal men throughout a string of disastrous relationships. Yet, strangely, that violent past has driven her into a relationship based on pain.

Viola's own sick and elderly mother encouraged her to become a full-time slave to Mistress Mir, who was an old family friend. 'My mother was very seriously ill in hospital but she sensed that I needed to be controlled and looked after by someone who really cared. She actually picked Mir for me. She understood my weaknesses and considered that Mir would actually improve the quality and happiness of my life.'

Just hours after meeting Mir at her mother's hospital bedside, Viola and her mistress-to-be returned to Mir's self-equipped dungeon where Viola happily became a slave to her every whim and desire. 'From that day on, I realised my mom's face lit up whenever Mir showed up at the hospital. Whenever Mir wasn't around, Mom talked about her. She encouraged us.'

Viola speaks about her enslavement as if it were the most normal thing in the world. 'I am a genuine "S&M" pervert and being a slave helps me to fulfil my fantasies. I feel no shame.'

At the age of 44, Viola says she feels that her enslavement is more than just another example of sexual perversity. 'I live every aspect of my life as a slave. I feel no guilt because this is what I want.'

Part of that devotion to Mistress Mir entails being 'lent out' to other mistresses if Mir commands it. 'Viola is my property,' says Mir. 'If I decide that she should be tortured by others then that is entirely up to me.'

Mir explains her role as a mistress with pleasurable detachment. 'Being a dominatrix gives me control in most situations. These are not privileges that I use with indifference.'

Those 'privileges' include bondage, fetishes, feminisation and role playing. Says Mir, 'Equestrian, military, medical and historical scenes are just a few of the role-playing scenarios that I get into. I enjoy becoming the character that I play.'

Mir openly admits to using a favourite instrument of torture on Viola and the other part-time slaves who sometimes visit her home. 'It is a four-foot single-tailed signal whip. I love to use it because of the amount of control and skill the whip requires.' She even claims, 'I can swing the whip with my full arm's strength and still not cause harm.'

And Mir's slave, Viola, is no simple country girl entrapped in a life of degradation. She has a Bachelor's degree in teaching and insists that she has chosen this lifestyle.

But there have been a few close shaves along the way as she has encountered others whose demands are not quite as reasonable as those of Mistress Mir.

Once, a male dominant to whom Mir loaned Viola forced a needle filled with high-grade heroin into Viola's backside. She lost consciousness and had to go 'cold turkey' for a week to recover from the massive dose of narcotics. Another time she was almost suffocated during a dangerous bout of sexual activity and some of the beatings she has suffered have certainly scarred her for life.

But Viola is unrepentant. 'This is the life I have chosen. My mistress ultimately controls every aspect of my life. This is the way I want it to be. Many people will find it hard to understand what I am and certainly enslavement is something that should only occur on a voluntary basis.'

Remarkably, 90 per cent of Viola's typical day as a slave to Mistress Mir sounds very mundane. 'I make her breakfast, accompany her to appointments, pick up her children from school, help them with their homework, cook everyone supper and keep the house in good order,' she explains earnestly. 'I am her friend, bodyguard, assistant, lover, slave.'

At around midnight, almost every evening, Viola's apparently ordinary existence turns into something far more disturbing. 'That's when Madam decides it is time for danger, which means that severe physical punishment is likely to occur,' explains Viola.

That punishment usually involves a visit to Mistress Mir's dungeon, or 'playroom' as she calls it. The array of instruments of torture that line the walls of this plushly carpeted room include:

- Five closets where Mistress Mir often locks Viola

or any of her other part-time slaves for hours on end;
- A huge wooden cross, where slaves are often left hanging;
- Iron cages;
- Swings suspended from the ceiling; a king-size, leather four-poster bed, complete with built-in wrist and ankle restraints;
- A medieval-style rack;
- A throne where Mir often sits while barking orders to her slaves;
- A coffin in which some slaves are forced to lie.

'That playroom represents a heightened state of craziness when slaves like me are in the mood to be punished,' explains Viola.

And Mir positively beams with pride when talking about her playroom. 'I'm very proud of it. Everything in it was custom made for me. It is the dream dungeon. Many of the major pieces of bondage furniture in my playroom are works of art.

'The inquisitor's chair is copied from one I saw in a medieval museum of torture. The coffin was inspired by a trip I made to Egypt. The roasting chair was modelled on a chair used by witch hunters to force confessions by roasting the genitals of the person strapped to it.'

Three or four times a year Viola's mistress hosts parties at her rambling house where 'anything goes', lasting for two days. But probably one of the most bizarre aspects of Viola's life as a sex slave is that she was recently the victim of a kidnap attempt by an African millionaire businessman. 'This guy decided that he wanted to take me back to Africa and keep me for ever, but I wanted to stay with Mir,' explains Viola.

After many weeks of negotiation, the businessman eventually abandoned his plans to snatch Viola.

But then last year, a wealthy diplomat at the United Nations in New York offered Mir half-a-million dollars to 'buy' Viola and keep her as his full-time slave. Once again, her devotion to her current mistress took precedence and the offer was politely declined. Viola adds, 'It was very flattering, but I am happy living and working for Mir. I don't want any other master or mistress.'

Her mistress says that while there is inevitably a level of humiliation involved in how she treats Viola, 'Humiliation differs from person to person. There are too many shades of grey in these situations for me to say whether or not I can, or will, humiliate anyone.

'My personal code of ethics is simple. I treat my slaves with respect. They are all valued for their individuality. I will do nothing to jeopardise myself or the well-being of my slave.'

And Viola's devotion to her mistress is unquestioning. 'Madam is an incredible woman. And by God's good grace, we'll never be apart from each other again.'

Appendix

*'It is not the whip that makes men, but the lure of
things that are worthy to be loved.'*

Woodrow Wilson, 1906

Further Cases

In addition to the cases already described in vivid detail
in *Women in Chains*, these examples provide even further
evidence that, as we rapidly approach the next century,
the enslavement of women continues in many different
forms.

Britain

• Maria Gomez, aged 30, was brought to Britain by a
Palestinian and his wife who forced her into a life of
slavery. She finally escaped from their clutches but only
after enduring beatings and verbal abuse and a wage of
just £2 a week (1991).

• Anita Reyes had to escape from her employers by tying bedsheets together and climbing out of her second-floor bedroom window in the centre of London. She had been regularly beaten by the wife of her employer (1992).

• Lulu's employer was a British army major serving abroad in Brunei. She returned to Britain with the family. But she was ordered to sleep at the end of her master's bed whenever his wife was away visiting friends and relatives in the country and endured regular beatings and sexual abuse. She eventually escaped but was too frightened to press charges against the family (1993).

• Cindy Dindial was slapped, kicked, punched and beaten with a rolling pin and tied up virtually every day of her employment, by two evil doctors in the historic English city of Lincoln. After six months of non-stop torture and abuse, Cindy courageously walked out with nothing but the clothes she stood in and went to the police. Both doctors were jailed after being convicted of assault and causing actual bodily harm. It was a very rare case of prosecution as a result of a complaint by a domestic slave (1993).

• Brett Mills, aged 34, from Croydon, south London, imprisoned a twelve-year-old girl in an apartment as his sex slave and then subjected her to an appalling series of attacks. He was found guilty of various sex crimes and imprisoned for fifteen years (1995).

• Ruthless madam Myra Ling-Ling Forde lured schoolgirls who were living in care into working as prostitutes for her and then trapped them against their will. She was eventually arrested and sentenced to six years in jail (1995).

Brazil
• Women slaves are being hired by the dozen in the Amazon frontier town of Maraba. Police occasionally raid ranches where they are being held captive but there are rarely prosecutions of the offending land owners (1990).
• Geralda Santos was held as a slave for two years in a town in the north of the country. She was made to sleep in the garden, given only one meal a day and forbidden to keep her child with her (1995).

Canada
• Paul Bernardo, an accountant, was found guilty of murdering two schoolgirls he had enslaved in his bungalow in St Catherine's, Ontario. He was convicted on nine charges including first-degree murder, kidnappings, confinements and rape (1995).

Ghana
• Thousands of girls are being forced into menial and sexual slavery by being given away as Tro-kasi's — the term means 'fetish slave' — to single men. Their families in remote villages believe they will improve a run of bad luck by allowing their children to be enslaved (1995).

India
• Up to 50,000 Nepalese girls are believed to be

currently enslaved in brothels in Bombay. Most of them are working to repay the price their families were paid for them (1995).

• Little Ameena Begum was sold by her father to a wealthy Arab sheikh when she was just ten years old. 60-year-old Yahya al-Sagish paid $4,000 (£2,700) and was then caught trying to smuggle little Ameena through an airport from where he planned to board a jet for Saudi Arabia. It even transpired that al-Sagish had already 'married' the little girl in a wedding ceremony in India and planned to use her as his sex slave for the rest of his life. After Yahya's arrest, police discovered photographs of four other girls in his possession. It is understood he had a harem of women waiting for him back in Saudi Arabia. He was jailed for a year (1990).

Italy

• Maria-Rosano Rota, aged 31, was kept locked in a bedroom for seventeen years by parents who thought the world too evil for her. She was found after a Mother Superior tipped off police in Colnago, northern Italy (1995).

Japan

• Former female prisoners of war finally gained some recognition for their plight during World War II when hundreds of them were kept as so-called 'comfort women' in prison brothels controlled by the Japanese armed forces. The Japanese government agreed to consider compensation payments to the surviving women (1995).

Kuwait/Britain

• For three years Alice Santos was abused by her Kuwaiti employers. She finally escaped when the family took her to London on a vacation. But she believes to this day that her life is in danger because she has dared to speak out against her former employers (1992).

Morocco

• Girls as young as twelve are working gruelling 55-hour weeks in sweltering temperatures in a factory in Meknes. Many of the garments produced end up on the shelves of some of Britain's best-known chain stores (1992).

Nigeria/Britain

• Roseline Tigani, aged fifteen, was sold for £2 to an English couple from Sheffield, in the north of England. She was forced to work eighteen hours a day as a servant and made to kneel at her master and mistress's bedroom door every night. Roseline eventually escaped, took her former employers to court and was awarded £20,000 in damages However, the British Home Office deported her immediately after her court victory because she had illegally overstayed her visa (1990).

Pakistan

• Tens of thousands of workers are being held in various forms of slavery, according to the latest findings from the

Human Rights Watch charity in Asia. The group say that women are being forced into slave-labour camps to work as carpet-weavers (1995).

Sierra Leone

• Adama Bangura was just sixteen when her parents sold her to a businessman in Abidjan. She was then transported to the Lebanon as a slave, where she was trapped against her will for three years before finally escaping back to her home country (1990).

South Africa

• Jabulile Masuka, aged seventeen, was seriously assaulted by the man who purchased her, as well as the agent who sold her after she was secretly transported across the border from Mozambique to villages in the Komatipoort area of Eastern Transvaal (1990).

Spain

• Sofia was taken from her village in south-east Spain to Valencia when she was just twelve years old, and was sold to a Lebanese family by her father in exchange for $50 (£35). When she was seventeen and enslaved in Madrid, Sofia befriended a woman who persuaded her to run away. She started working as a prostitute to survive. But she still preferred life on the streets to life inside that demonic family. She is still working as a prostitute and her abusers have never been brought to justice (1994).

Switzerland

• Teresa worked in Kuwait as a domestic for the al-Sabah royal family When news of the Iraqi invasion reached them, she was abandoned by her employers and taken to the royal palace in Kuwait City She eventually escaped to the family's home in Switzerland, where she was raped and beaten by one teenage prince. No action was ever taken against the al-Sabah family (1991).

United Arab Emirates

• Sixteen-year-old Filipina slave Sarah Balabagan had her death sentence commuted to 100 lashes after stabbing to death a member of the household who was raping her (1995).

United States of America

• Los Angeles businessman Nasim Mussry and his sister Elsa Singman were accused of selling sixty women into involuntary servitude to people who paid $3,000 (£2,000) each to use them as domestic servants (1985).

• Dayna Broussard, aged eight, was beaten to death by members of a commune at their isolated farmhouse in Sandy, near Portland, Oregon. She had been kept enslaved along with fifty-three other children at the property (1991).

• Rima, just nineteen, endured severe beatings at the hands of her employer even after moving from Saudi Arabia to the glamorous city of Los Angeles. The beautiful Indian girl was threatened with death if she uttered a word about her enslavement (1993).

COMING SOON FROM **BLAKE'S TRUE CRIME LIBRARY**

THE MURDER OF RACHEL NICKELL
The truth about the tragic murder on Wimbledon
Common
Mike Fielder

CAGED HEAT
The true stories of what really goes on behind the bars of
women's prisons
Wensley Clarkson

SUNDAY BLOODY SUNDAY
Amazing true crime stories from the *News of the World*'s
Sunday magazine
Drew Makenzie

BROTHERS IN BLOOD
The true story of the brothers who killed their parents
Tim Brown and Paul Cheston

THE MAN WHO KILLED SUZY LAMPLUGH
The inside story of one of our most enduring mysteries
Chris Berry-Dee

YOU COULD WIN THE AMAZING SLEUTH'S SILVER DAGGER!

The first twelve titles in Blake's True Crime Library series each contain a question relating to the book. Collect the numbered editions of Blake's True Crime Library, and when you have the answers to all the questions, fill in the form which you will find at the back of the twelfth book and send it to Blake Publishing to be entered into a prize draw.

HERE IS THE NINTH QUESTION
In which capital city did Laxmi Peria Swami lead a life of slavery?
The winner will receive the exclusive sleuth's silver dagger and five runners-up will receive three free copies of Blake's True Crime Library titles.

How To Enter
Fill in the answer form contained in the twelfth book in the series and post it to us. If you have won, we will notify you. Whether you are a winner or not, you will still be eligible for a *FREE* True Crime newsletter!

Competition Rules
1.   The 'How to Enter' instructions form part of the rules.
2.   These competitions are not open to any members of Blake Publishing or their families, or Blake Publishing's advertising agents, printers or distributors.
3.   The prizes will be awarded in order of their value, to the senders of the first winning entries after the closing date.
4.   Entries must be on the entry coupon supplied and will not be accepted after the closing date.
5.   No claim is necesary, winners will be notified.
6.   In cases where a manufacturer discontinues a product which has been specified as a prize, Blake Publishing Ltd will substitute the nearest equivalent model of similar or higher value.
7.   The Editor's decision is final, and no correspondence can be entered into.

BEAT THE RUSH!
ORDER YOUR COPIES OF FORTHCOMING TRUE CRIME TITLES DIRECTLY.

Simply fill in the form below, and we will send you your books as they become available.

Name: ....

Address: ....

....

....

Daytime tel.: ....

Card (please tick as appropriate)

Visa ☐   Mastercard ☐

Access ☐   Switch ☐

Card number: ....

Expiry date: ....

For Switch cards only

Issue date ....   Issue number ....

Please send me *(tick as appropriate)*

☐ Deadlier than the Male
Wensley Clarkson
☐ Natural Born Killers
Kate Kray
☐ In the Company of Killers
Norman Parker
☐ The Spanish Connection
John Lightfoot
☐ Deadly Affair
Nicolas Davies
☐ Doctors who Kill
Wensley Clarkson
☐ Vigilante
Ron Farebrother
☐ The Man who Killed Suzy
Lamplugh
Chris Berry-Dee

☐ The Female of the
Species
Wensley Clarkson
☐ Women in Chains
Wensley Clarkson
☐ The Murder of Rachel
Nickell
Mike Fielder
☐ Caged Heat
Wensley Clarkson
☐ Sunday Bloody Sunday
Drew Mackenzie
☐ Brothers in Blood
Tim Brown and Paul Cheston

All titles are £4.99. Postage and packing are free. No money will be deducted from your card until the books become available.